FLYING BOATS
& SEAPLANES

In memory of Ralph Evain

Published 1998 by Bay View Books Ltd
The Red House
25-26 Bridgeland Street
Bideford
Devon EX39 2PZ

© Copyright ETAI, Paris 1996
English translation © Copyright Bay View Books Ltd 1998

English translation by Robin Sawers

ISBN 1 901432 20 3

Printed in Spain

FLYING BOATS & SEAPLANES

A History from 1905

Stéphane Nicolaou

WITH THANKS TO

Alice Evain, Anick Evain, Geneviève Laloux

Jacques Borgé, Jean Delmas, Jean Devaux, Claude Evain, René J. Francillon, Steve Ginter, Gérard Gorokoff, Jean Guigui, Marcelin Hodeir, Sandy Jones, Herbert Léonard, B.J. Long, Michel Marrand, Michel Marani, Robert C. Mikesh, Gerhardt Müller.

And to the following organizations: Air France, Canadair, Caproni, Claudius Dornier, Convair, Curtiss, Dornier, Douglas, Grumman, Hughes, Lockheed, Macchi, Martin, Pan Am, Shin Meïwa, Short, Sikorsky, S.H.A.A., and in particular the Musée de l'Air et de l'Espace.

C O N T E N T S

Introduction

Marine aviation has a special place in the history of flying. In spite of the difficulties encountered by its pioneers, it soon became a sporting activity which had evident military possibilities. It experienced a considerable upsurge during the First World War, with seaplanes involved in all types of aerial missions in spite of their lack of aerodynamic efficiency, which was due as much to the shape of the fuselage as to the presence of floats. This then led to the rapid development of the seaplane in the interwar years.

During the 1920s and 1930s the racing seaplanes of the Schneider Trophy era were able to achieve much higher speeds than landplanes because they were able to use very much longer takeoff runs. Seaplanes explored parts of the world inaccessible to their land-based counterparts, and, towards the end of the thirties, giant flying boats opened up regular passenger routes across the oceans connecting America with the other continents.

The Second World War radically altered the outlook for marine aviation, as none of the designers succeeded in perfecting an effective bomber or fighter seaplane. Sea patrols were eventually undertaken by landplanes, and the small reconnaissance seaplanes carried by the larger fighting ships disappeared. Air sea rescue was the only new task allotted specifically to seaplanes, and many remarkable feats were achieved in this sphere.

After the war, since aero engines had become much more reliable, there was no longer a real need to use flying boats for safety reasons on the long transoceanic routes, and in addition the number of airfields grew rapidly. As a result, marine aviation only continued in a minor role, its history restricted to a few machines which seldom proceeded beyond the prototype stage. Finally, flying boats gave way to helicopters even for air sea rescue.

Be that as it may, there are some parts of the world where, even today, seaplanes are still the main form of air transport. Ralph Evain's evocative colour photographs have captured with a poetic eye these last survivors of a bygone age.

CHAPTER 1

Early Days

MARINE AVIATION HAD A SLOW AND DIFFICULT BIRTH. FROM THE END OF THE 19TH CENTURY ONWARDS, OVER THREE CONTINENTS, BOLD ENGINEERS AND MECHANICS SET OUT ON THE QUEST FOR THE BOAT THAT FLIES

Louis Blériot and Gabriel Voisin joined forces to design Blériot III, which was tested, without success, on Lake Enghien in May 1906.

Henri Brégi leaves Monaco harbour in 1914 on a Breguet B2, one of the first

arine aviation had a slow and difficult birth. From the end of the 19th century onwards, over three continents, bold engineers and mechanics in search of new sensations set out on the quest for the boat that flies.

In 1876 the French pioneer Alphonse Pénaud filed the first patent for a flying machine with a boat hull, provided with retractable landing gear at the end of the wings. An unpiloted glider fitted with two floats was produced in the United States by Gallaudet in 1897, but the credit for the creation of the first seaplane goes to the Austrian Wilhelm Kress.

In 1898, at the age of 62, he raised the money for the *Drachenflieger*, a triplane in tandem, with its wing surface material stretched over a steel frame, resting on two large floats. The 30hp Daimler engine drove two broad propellers. This was the first time that a flying machine of any kind had been fitted with a petrol engine. The power obtained was insufficient to lift the 1870lb machine, all the more so as the aluminium floats had not been designed to cope with its great bulk. On October 3rd 1901 the *Drachenflieger* was launched on the reservoir in the Vienna Woods near Tullnerbach. One of the floats tore off at the top, and the machine sank. In spite of this spectacular failure, Kress persevered, constructing a similar seaplane with greater wing area. Its frame was completed in 1903, but due to lack of money Kress had to abandon his project.

At the same time in the Antipodes, the Australian Lawrence Hargrave, following completely opposite principles, designed a very light steam-driven catamaran, but this was abandoned before it had even been fitted with wings.

The year 1903 ended with the first flight of the Wright brothers' *Flyer* in the United States on December 17th. Less than two years later they succeeded in completing a flight lasting more than half an hour. Aviation had arrived, but marine aviation had still to be invented.

On June 6th 1905 Gabriel Voisin became the first man to take off from and touch down on a stretch of water, using a glider towed by a motorboat. The glider resembled a kite of the Hargrave type mounted on two floats. After construction at Billancourt, it was launched on the Seine and hitched up to the racing launch *La Rapière* with Alphonse Tellier at the helm. A dynamometer was fitted to the cable, while an anemometer indicated the wind speed, which made it possible to establish how much power would be needed to enable the glider to take off. With a firm hand on the controls, Gabriel Voisin waited until the machine had gathered speed and then operated the elevator. The glider took off without hesitation and after flying for 150 yards settled at about 60 feet, level with the tops of the poplars that line the river. Two further tests took place on the same day, with flights of approximately 50 and 600 yards.

Immediately after this exploit Gabriel and Charles Voisin met Louis Blériot, who asked them to produce a machine with an engine, made up of two frames in the form of an ellipse placed in tandem. The whole assembly floated on the water with the aid of skids surrounded by tapering sealed tubes. Christened *Blériot III*, this seaplane was tested without success on Lake Enghien in May 1906. Accepting the Voisin brothers' suggestions, Blériot only kept the rear part of this machine in his *Blériot IV*, which was fitted with conventional biplane wings and proper floats. On October 18th 1906 taxiing tests only resulted in a speed of 19mph, which was insufficient for takeoff. The 24hp Antoinette engine was nowhere near powerful enough, and this led the partners to give up their project for good. However the idea of making an aeroplane take off from water resulted in some pretty harebrained solutions, such as the machine built by Barton and Rawson in 1905 on the Isle of Wight, the multiplane of Israel Ludlow shown without engine at the Jamestown exhibition in the United States in 1907, Ravaud's 'aéroscaphe' which took part in the Monaco competition in 1909, and the Waterplane of Humphrey, who was nicknamed 'the mad dentist' by his fellow citizens in Wivenhoe, Essex – not without reason.

In a more serious vein, in the United States in November 1908 the Glenn Curtiss Aerodrome no. 3 *June Bug*, which had already flown with conventional landing gear, was converted into a seaplane by fitting two wooden floats covered in canvas. In the course of tests carried out on Lake Keuka near Hammondsport, the machine, renamed *The Loon*, reached a speed of 25mph, but the hydrodynamic drag was too great for a takeoff to be realistically possible.

While these experiments were taking place, a young man was working to solve the specific problems of aerodynamics, hydrodynamics and engines in seaplane design.

**Wilhelm Kress's *Drachenflieger*
afloat on the
Tullnerbach lake in 1901.**
It was the first seaplane in history.

In October 1906, *Blériot IV* with its two Antoinette engines tried to take off from the water, but did not manage to exceed a speed of 19mph.

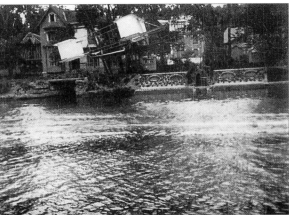

Towed by the launch *La Rapière*, **Gabriel Voisin takes off on June 6th 1905 from the the River Seine.**

Jean Bécu in full flight at Monaco in April 1911 on the third example of the Fabre seaplane.

THE GREAT PIONEERS

Henri Fabre

Born in Marseilles in 1882, Henri Fabre had the good fortune to belong to a family of very rich ship-owners. Passionately interested in everything to do with the sea, his enthusiasm led him to take up engineering, and he took his engineer's diploma at the École supérieure d'électricité in 1906. His father, Augustin Fabre, gave him 100,000 francs to build a seaplane and a systematic programme of tests was successfully carried out from a steamboat, the *Essor*, on the Étang de Berre.

Aerodynamic tests were carried out in a steady wind on flat or curved wing surfaces of up to 170sq ft, while other tests used kites which rose to a height of 1000 feet where they launched model aeroplanes in order to study their stability.

A large catamaran towed by the *Essor* was used for the hydrodynamic tests, but an accident off Marseilles led Henri Fabre to choose an alternative: a float with a flexible underside comprising a sheet of plywood functioning in the manner of a drum skin. The tests showed that due to its shape, with a flat surface below and a cylindrical surface above, this type of float only interacts with the water when it is immersed.

The Fabre propeller was fitted to a Renault car with a 14hp engine. It was technically remarkable in that it had variable pitch.

Eventually, on April 9th 1909, the curé of Martigues blessed a strange vessel minus its three 12hp Anzani engines. The machine underwent its first independent tests in the harbour of La Mède on July 8th 1909. Unfortunately the floats, the underside of which was turned up at the front, dug into the water and prevented the seaplane from reaching its takeoff speed. Weighing 484lb, the engines were much too heavy given the low power produced, not to mention the complexity of their transmission systems. Only the general idea of the three floats, two at the front and one at the back, was to be re-used successfully on other seaplanes.

The large sum Henri Fabre had been given was almost exhausted when Laurent Seguin came up with his Gnome seven-cylinder rotary engine, which gave an output of 50hp with a weight of less than 150lb. Along with all the other flying enthusiasts, the young Fabre went to the Rheims Aviation Week in August 1909. There he met Charles Gavoty, a friend of his father, who suggested that he should buy two of the Gnome engines with which Henry Farman had just enjoyed such success. One was to be fitted to the seaplane, and to get the money back the other was to be sold later at a profit of 3000 francs, which would cover most of the initial investment.

For some time Henri Fabre had been a great friend of Laurent and Augustin Seguin. One day the latter brought along a scale model with a rubber-band motor, which had wings at the rear and a horizontal stabilizer at the front, a configuration which was later to be christened the Canard ('duck'). Longitudinal stability was achieved automatically by setting the front stabilizer at a greater angle than the wings. Delighted with the simplicity of the arrangement, the two friends produced a Canard glider, while Henri Fabre built a small seaplane with a wing area of 108sq ft. On December 24th 1909 the single Anzani engine continued to prove very inadequate. The pilot executed a manoeuvre when coming to a stop that caused the machine to capsize; he escaped with a cold dip. However, the Canard configuration was not to blame for the accident.

The seaplane with a wing area of 258sq ft was fitted with its Gnome engine at the end of January 1910. On March 27th 1910 a first straight line test showed that the machine was ready to take off; success was very near, but it was still necessary to balance the torque of the engine to eliminate a worrying tendency to slew round.* Henri Fabre invited his father and Laurent and Augustin Seguin for the great day.

On March 28th 1910 the machine was ready. In ideally calm weather, it was towed by the *Essor* towards the middle of the Étang de Berre and then brought alongside with its tail to the steamboat's side, the propeller being within arm's reach for the crew to start the engine. *"Surrounded on all sides by open space, I set off at great speed. On this calm, mirror-like surface, our progress is delightfully smooth and gentle; the rotary engine being so far from me, I am not even aware of the vibration.*

For a long time I continue this rapid taxiing without opening the throttles fully and thus risking takeoff. I then return to the boat to reflect calmly on this initial achievement.

I have never been on an aircraft before, either as a passenger or as a pilot, so I cannot rely on my instinctive reactions, but my machine has been designed to have automatic stability, and in this perfectly calm weather I should be able to fly without altering the controls, so I decide that to start with I will only operate the throttles.

With my hand on the throttle lever, I let the machine accelerate away; one of the rear floats rises, so I slow down and by

* Equivalent to a 180º spin due to an uncontrolled skid on the road

Henri Fabre with the Gnome engine of his seaplane at Monaco in 1911.

On March 28th 1910 Henri Fabre moves away from the *Essor* for his first takeoff. Due to the speed, only the rear tips of the floats are resting on the surface.

Jean Bécu at Monaco aboard Henri Fabre's strange trimaran on April 12th 1911.

The three-engined Fabre on test on July 8th 1909. The badly designed floats are digging into the water.

adjusting the neutral point of the warp am able to alter the relative inclination of the two wings. I accelerate again, and this time both rear floats rise up. I am in the air, perfectly stable; whether gliding across this oily sea or buzzing along a dozen feet above it in the still atmosphere, the impression is the same. Throttling back, I soon see the front float gently pressing down on the water, leaving a fine trace like that of a diamond on a sheet of glass.

I take off again, making each flight longer than the last, going into wide sweeping turns in the air. No sudden movements, no shocks when touching down on the water. My machine does not cause me the least apprehension, and when I board the boat again the onlookers reckon that I have a really smooth craft, whose gentle movements give no cause for concern. Laurent Seguin declares that the most urgent matter is to have the achievement officially recorded. So that afternoon, since there are now some small waves on the Étang de Berre, I make two takeoffs in the harbour of La Mède watched by Monsieur Bazin and a bailiff, flanked by two gendarmes."

Thus Henri Fabre achieved success. He was the first man to take off from and touch down on water in an aircraft, yet he remained modest and made no attempt to conceal the faults of his machine, whose excessive inertia made it difficult to handle. A few weeks after his exploit, he got into a series of uncontrollable swerves and fell with his machine from a height of about 130 feet. The accident was not serious and this confirmed the relative safety of flying over water.

helped to overcome the suction of the water on the floats. Curtiss successfully developed various floats with the assistance of Lieutenant T.G. Ellyson, a submariner placed at his disposal by the U.S. Navy.

A second machine, based on a Type III airframe and fitted with a tractor propeller, enabled Curtiss to pay a visit to Captain Charles F. Pond, commander of the *U.S.S. Pennsylvania*, on February 17th. The aircraft was lifted on board together with its pilot, who helped in the manoeuvre. After a conversation with the captain, Curtiss returned to North Island in his seaplane. This was an important occasion, because he had fulfilled the requirements laid down by the U.S. Navy for financing the development of seaplanes.

Without wasting any time, Curtiss went back to the pusher configuration, fitting a float on which he mounted three retractable wheels. With this machine he took off from North Island on February 25th 1911 and reached Coronado Beach, where he landed in a conventional manner on the beach.

After a good meal at a seaside hotel, he took off again from the hard sand, landing in the water in front of his hangars and returning to them under his own power. The first amphibian in aeronautical history had just proved its ability to manoeuvre on land and sea as well as in the air.

The following year, the American constructor devoted himself to the study of the seaplane with a floating hull, known in the English-speaking world as a flying boat to distinguish it from the other type of seaplane called a float-plane, where only the floats are in contact with the water.

Named *Flying boat no.1*, the first model produced by Curtiss

Glenn Curtiss aboard one of his machines.

Anthony James' Curtiss Tractor flying above the Mississippi during a flight of more than 1850 miles.

Glenn Curtiss

In the United States, Glenn Curtiss, who had visited Fabre at the time of the Second Aeronautical Exhibition in December 1910, was intensely interested in the problems of marine aviation. In fact in the spring of 1910 he had put down his *Albany Flier* on the waters of Lake Keuka, proving in the process the efficacy of some emergency buoyancy material, which he fortunately did not need on his later flight from Albany to New York on May 29th the same year.

His aim now was to develop a real seaplane. Starting with a Pusher airframe, he added to it a central float that was wider than it was long, with a second smaller one at the front, then a hydrofoil (as a water shield) mounted in front of the pilot to protect him from the spray as well as to damp any tendency to dive; it was also intended to provide additional aerodynamic lift.

On January 26th 1911, the machine took off from North Island in San Diego Bay thanks to a slightly choppy sea which

was tested for the first time on January 10th 1912, but without success, since he did not manage to take off. The very wide hull looked like a float and contained the engine, from which rose two chains for driving the two side propellers, the two-seater (side-by-side) cockpit being placed behind the engine.

Flying boat no. 2, nicknamed *The Flying Fish,* returned to a more usual layout apart from the hull, which extended over its whole length and now supported the tailplane.

In the first tests carried out at Hammondsport, *The Flying Fish* obstinately refused to take off. Numerous modifications made no difference. Finally Curtiss followed the machine in a motorboat in order to watch the behaviour of the hull and the water flow both at low and high speeds. Back on dry land, he

asked a carpenter to make two wedge-shaped blocks of wood, which he fixed under the hull slightly behind the centre of gravity. This step kept half of the hull out of contact with the water at about the speed needed for takeoff; as a result it also made it possible to achieve a degree of rotation which opened the angle of incidence, thus increasing lift on takeoff. If the rear section of the hull sank into the water, however, the speed would immediately drop.

It was in July 1912 that *The Flying Fish* demonstrated the advantages of the step, and Curtiss reckoned he had invented the seaplane with a hull. Unfortunately he was two months too late to be considered the first, as there was no shortage of innovators in France.

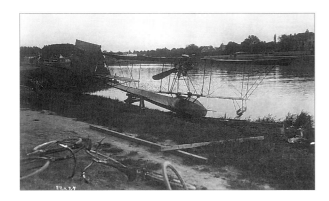

François Denhaut

In 1911, François Denhaut, chief pilot at Pierre Levasseur's flying school, designed a seaplane with a hull. It was really the first aircraft of this type to show the way forward for marine aviation. The hull was shaped like a triangle with the point at the top and fitted with Forlanini-type lift-off plates intended to give hydrodynamic lift. The Gnome 50hp engine, similar to Fabre's, drove a pusher propeller, the whole unit being placed between the biplane wings, high up and well behind the pilot. A fixed undercarriage with two wheels made it possible to manoeuvre on the ground, and allowed Denhaut to test his aircraft by taking off from the ground.

On March 12th 1912, the pilot and constructor took off from Port-Aviation, flew over the River Seine and decided to come down on it but he failed to straighten up the machine in time and the plates dug in under the water. Suddenly braked, the flying boat flipped over on its back. Denhaut, who was fortunately wearing an inflatable jacket, escaped from the cockpit and took refuge on the hull. The badly damaged machine was hoisted onto the bank.

François Denhaut decided to rebuild it, making important modifications. The hull, which tended to sink into the water due to its very slender shape, was now made rectangular in section and thus flat-bottomed, with a flat stepped caisson level with the undercarriage axle, inclined at an angle of four degrees to the horizontal. This transformation was entirely due to the intervention of Robert Duhamel, who had warned Denhaut that in its original form the hull would be inefficient due to the lack of a step.

The machine was first tried out on a stretch of water behind Port-Aviation. The wheels were temporarily replaced with wing floats. On April 13th 1912 the seaplane took off from Juvisy airfield and landed close to the Seine on such muddy ground that the undercarriage broke. After a gentle launch into the water, Denhaut took off and alighted seven or eight times, before coming down on the Seine and returning to the bank. The first seaplane with a hull, or flying boat, had flown.

This was an important occasion, since unlike the Fabre machine and the Curtiss amphibian, François Denhaut's machine can be seen as the prototype of a very long line of flying boats, of which several thousand were built under various names.

RACES, COMPETITIONS AND MEETINGS

Monaco 1912

The possibility of fitting floats to proven airframes resulted in a rapid increase in the number of types of marine aircraft, especially in France. Aviation experts agreed that these machines were only suitable for recreational use, with takeoffs from a really calm surface, and there were numerous sceptics regarding their use in rough water, particularly in the traditionally conservative circles of the Navy. In order to convince the doubters and at the same time stimulate research, a series of richly endowed meetings were organized.

Georges Prade, secretary of the Monaco committee, suggested the setting up of a seaplane competition for the year 1912. The tests, from March 24th to March 31st 1912, comprised:

– a takeoff and touchdown in calm conditions (one point for each);

– a takeoff and touchdown in rough water (worth respectively two and three points);

– a takeoff followed by a touchdown on the water, then coming ashore on a beach in such a manner that the pilot is able to get out "without jumping to reach the ground and without touching the water" (four points);

– a departure from the beach, with the pilot getting into his seat "without getting his feet wet".

Eight competitors entered with six different machines. The participation of Hugh Robinson, an engineer from Curtiss piloting

a Triad, made the event international in character.

The first day, which was dominated by Jules Fischer on a Henry Farman, was marked by the crash of the Canard-Voisin of Maurice Colliex, happily without any serious consequences for the pilot, who was flying again two days later, sharing with Paul Rugère. Fischer gained points in all the tests and got a bonus for passengers. Unfortunately the second Canard-Voisin was eliminated the following day. On March 30th Benoît's Sanchez-Besa hit a wreck with its right-hand float, and his machine capsized. The final overall results were as follows:

First, Fischer with 112.10 points; second, Renaux with 100.80 points; third, Paulhan with 86.30 points; fourth, Robinson with 71.90 points; fifth, Caudron with 65 points; sixth, Benoît with 50.30 points; seventh Rugère and Colliex with 41.75 points.

Although still in its infancy, the seaplane had shown some pretty surprising abilities. The Maurice-Farman of Eugène Renaux, for instance, completed more than 200 sorties without the slightest mechanical trouble. The same machine negotiated an eight-foot swell without any particular difficulty in the taxiing manoeuvres.

However, it must be pointed out that over the whole event men and machines benefited from excellent weather conditions and from particularly docile seas. Be that as it may, Alphonse Tellier ended his report on the Monaco Hydro-aeroplane Competition with the following words: "The results were not only very good and encouraging, but I would even say unexpected".

Jules Fischer, leaning on the wing of his Farman, watches the Canard-Voisin being launched at Monaco on March 24th 1912.

Jean Benoît on the seaplane built by Sanchez Besa, an engineer of Chilean origin.

Piloted by Paul Rugère, the Canard-Voisin in full flight at Monaco in March 1912 (opposite page).

René Caudron moves his machine away from the shore under its his own power. The rear float is of the Fabre type.

Robinson's Curtiss Triad (below) demonstrates its amphibious qualities. He is followed by the Caudron, piloted by its constructor.

Maurice Farman's seaplane (below right), piloted by Eugène Renaux, had large wheels mounted on the floats.

ENTRIES FOR THE HYDRO-AEROPLANE COMPETITION - MONACO MARCH 24-31 1912

1	Louis Paulin	Paulhan-Curtiss Triad	Curtiss 75hp	Curtiss floats
2	Hugh Robinson	Curtiss Triad	Curtiss 75hp	Curtiss floats
3	Maurice Colliex	Canard-Voisin	Canton-Unné 70hp	Fabre floats
4	Paul Rugère	Canard-Voisin	Anzani 70hp	Fabre floats
5	Eugène Renaux	Maurice-Farman biplane	Renault 70hp	Fabre floats
6	Jean Benoît	Sanchez-Besa biplane	Canton-Unné 110hp	Tellier floats
7	René Caudron	Caudron-Fabre biplane	Anzani 60hp	Fabre floats
8	Jules Fischer	Henry Farman biplane	Gnome 70hp	Farman floats

Under the attentive eye of Louis Paulhan, mechanics adjust the control surfaces on the nose of the Triad.

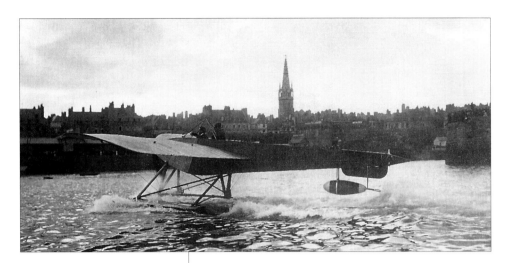

On August 26th 1912 the American Charles Weymann in a Nieuport was the winner of the St Malo-Jersey race.

The Train, presented at St Malo, used the same principles as the microlight which was to follow many years later.

St Malo 1912

The second big meeting, organized this time by the Aeronautical Commission of the Automobile-Club de France, took place at St Malo from August 24th-26th 1912. Twelve competitors entered and nine started, four of them on machines completely different from those that had taken part in the Monaco event. The presence of three monoplanes was particularly notable, and was a first.

The first test took place on August 24th in unfavourable weather conditions. It involved covering the route from St Malo to Grand-Jardin twice. A system of time bonuses made it possible to take into account the number of passengers accompanying the pilot. Labouret on the Astra C.M. was the winner, his actual time being improved considerably by the presence of two passengers on board; Busson on an 80hp Deperdussin only carried one passenger and was placed second, while Molla on his own covered the course in 13mins 37sec, the fastest actual time of all the competitors, with the aid of his 80hp R.E.P. Renaux and Benoît followed in the next places. Frank Barra's Sanchez-Besa turned back after the start, caught by a gust of wind. Charles Weymann touched down close to a torpedo boat which picked him up together with his Nieuport

The next day, the race over the route St Malo-Rochebonne-Le Décollé-St Malo was marked by two accidents: René Mesguisch had to come down on land as a result of engine failure and was quite seriously injured. His Paulhan-Curtiss was reduced to a wreck. Busson on the other hand touched down on the sea too fast, his 80hp Deperdussin turned over, and he and his passengers got off with a soaking. Benoît on his Sanchez-Besa won thanks to his three passengers, since his actual time of 20mins 30sec was reduced to 9min 14sec. Labouret came second with two passengers (actual time: 16min 9sec), and Molla was

third with a time of 15min 9sec, the course like that of the previous day measuring 14 miles.

On August 26th, flying with a crosswind and in the rain, the competitors fought it out over a course crossing the open sea from St Malo to Jersey via the Chausey islands and back, representing a total of 90 miles. For the first time a monoplane was the winner, Weymann with one passenger having his actual time of 2hrs 10min cut to 1hr 26min. He came in ahead of Labouret, Benoît and Molla, who (again on his own) went briefly off course.

Prizes were awarded for the cumulative results over the three days: Labouret was declared the overall winner and received 15,000 gold francs, as well as a bronze presented by the Navy minister. "It's nice to have the glory and all that as well", commented a reporter. Second man Benoît received 10,000 francs, while Molla in third place got 6,000 francs. The other awards went to Weymann, Renaux and Mesguisch.

The St Malo races proved that the seaplane had developed rapidly, its use no longer being dependent on the particularly favourable weather conditions of the Monaco event, and above all that the reliability of the machines and their engines permitted their use over the open sea. Although the Astra C.M., derived directly from a land-based machine shown at the 1911 military trials, was an aerodynamically well-tried design to which three Tellier floats without steps had been added, other participants had shown more daring by bringing monoplanes such as R.E.P., Nieuport and Deperdussin – even if they too had fitted floats to already proved airframes – or by using some unusual construction material, as Sanchez Besa had done, his biplane being made of steel tubes following the principles laid down by Gabriel Voisin.

A week before the St Malo meeting the competition at Geneva and the meeting at Boulogne-sur-Mer had taken place.

ENTRIES FOR THE SEAPLANE MEETING AT ST MALO AUGUST 24-26 1912

1	François Molla	R.E.P. monoplane	Gnome 80hp	R.E.P. floats
2	Émile Train	Astra-Train monoplane	Gnome 80hp	Train floats
3	Charles Weymann	Nieuport monoplane	Gnome 80hp	Nieuport floats
4	Jean Benoît	Sanchez-Besa biplane	Renault 100hp	Tellier floats
5	Paul Rugère	Sanchez-Besa biplane	Renault 70hp	Tellier floats
6	Marcel Chambenois	Borel monoplane	Gnome 80hp	Borel floats
7	André Beaumont	Donnet-Lévêque biplane type C	Gnome 80hp	Denhaut hull
8	Guillaume Busson	Deperdussin monoplane	Gnome 80hp	Tellier floats
9	Eugène Renaux	Maurice-Farman biplane	Renault 70hp	Fabre floats
10	René Labouret	Astra C.M. biplane	Renault 100hp	Tellier floats
11	René Mesguisch	Paulhan-Curtiss biplane	Paulhan-Curtiss 75hp	Curtiss floats
12	Frank Barra	Paulhan-Curtiss biplane	Paulhan-Curtiss 75hp	Curtiss floats

Labouret in the Astra C.M. was the winner of the St Malo races. The machine is seen here during launching tests on the banks of the Seine, prior to the competition. The configuration of the Astra C.M. was to become typical of the float-plane.

Swiss constructor Grandjean aboard the seaplane which he made and entered in the Geneva competition in August 1912.

Belgian pilot, Hélène Dutrieu (far right), the first woman to fly a seaplane, seen here on a 50hp Henry Farman on Lake Enghien in July 1912.

In August 1912 Léon Bourgeois became the first minister to fly in a seaplane (right), a Sommer without any creature comforts.

Other 1912 meetings

At Boulogne the weather was so dreadful that the demonstrations had to be postponed by one day, which did not prevent René Caudron, on August 16th, from making the first flight in his seaplane, which touched down on a very rough sea after a fine demonstration of manoeuvrability close to the crowd. On the same day, Marty, who was also trying to reach Boulogne from Le Crotoy, had to put down on the sea more than a mile from the shore, which he reached without any problems. The first day gave Labouchère on his Zodiac biplane a chance to thrill the crowd, which had been disappointed by René Caudron, who had broken his propeller; Marty saved the reputation of the Caudron firm by flying for half an hour. On August 18th only René Caudron made a flight, taking off from a rough sea and circling briefly above the crowd. At a height of 16 feet he switched off the ignition to descend in a tight turn, before landing on the shore in perfect safety. The final day became a disaster and proved that the sea-going qualities of the seaplanes were still inadequate. The Zodiac returned to port with its rear section broken before it had even taken off, while Marty and his

mechanic abandoned their Caudron, which was driven onto the beach by the current. René Caudron capsized but climbed onto one of the floats and directed salvage operations.

The Geneva seaplane competition attracted 30,000 people to the shores of Lake Geneva on April 19th. They had come to see André Beaumont, Frank Barra, René Grandjean and René Tétard, flying respectively a Donnet-Lévêque, a Paulhan-Curtiss, a Grandjean and a Sommer biplane. The next day, in spite of the wind and rain, they each made two flights.

The Lausanne international seaplane competition brought together René Caudron on his own biplane, Jean Dufour on a Sanchez-Besa biplane (Salmson 110hp engine), Tétard on a Sommer biplane (Salmson 110hp engine), René Grandjean on a Grandjean monoplane (Oerlikon 50hp engine) and Hélène Dutrieu on a Henry Farman biplane (Gnome 50hp engine).

The tests started at Ouchy. They comprised speed tests in the air and on the water, a takeoff from the water, a landing in a field 2½ miles away, then a return to the starting point. Everything went very well for the contestants: Tétard on the Sommer even made it from Geneva to Lausanne on September 1st in 37 minutes in a storm. On September 3rd Hélène Dutrieu, the first woman seaplane pilot, capsized with her underpowered machine, which was seriously damaged. She was quickly rescued.

In the summer of 1912 the lakes area attracted not only the Sommer, in which the constructor and Ernest Burri flew numerous important people, including on August 3rd the Minister of Labour Léon Bourgeois, but also the Sanchez-Besa, which, having demonstrated that it could carry five passengers, completed a series of excursions from Aix-les-Bains to a schedule organized by the Compagnie Transaérienne, starting on August 1st. This marks the beginning of the regular use of seaplanes with commercial applications in mind.

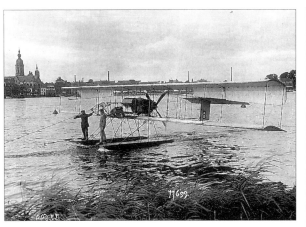

A general view of the Tamise meeting on the Scheldt (far left), with the Donnet-Lévêque (no. 10) and *The Train* (no.12) in the foreground, and the Sanchez-Besa (no.8) flying overhead.

The Sanchez-Besa of Jean Benoît emerged victorious from the Tamise trials in spite of numerous protests (left). The machine had a 70hp Renault engine.

Tamise 1912

The third and last large gathering of seaplanes in 1912 was the work of the Belgian Aero Club. It was held at Tamise on the Scheldt. Its aim was to establish which machine would be most suitable for colonial use, more particularly in the Congo which has large rivers as its arteries. The 15 competitors were placed according to the number of points won, which were awarded as follows:

– points for the competition, made up of the total time for the tests, the minimum distance before takeoff both with the current and against the current of the river, distance covered nonstop, and handling qualities on the water;

– a bonus for each passenger;

– points for additional features, including any facilities for covering the water in order to get back to the bank in case of engine failure, the possibility of starting the engine independently, the ability to come down on land, a flying speed in excess of 56mph, and whether the machine or the propeller are of metal.

The complexity of the points system gave rise to several complaints. Notwithstanding these, on April 3rd 1913 Benoît on a Sanchez-Besa biplane was declared the winner, closely followed by Georges Chemet on the Borel monoplane. The most striking fact was the international character of the entry: even if the German Büchow did not take part in the tests, Belgium was represented by two machines, the Jero biplane and the Lanser biplane, not forgetting the Paulhan-Curtisses of American origin. Of technical interest was the first appearance in a competition of a seaplane with a hull, which made the Tamise meeting really important. In fact André Beaumont's Donnet-Lévêque, which won the Roi des Belges Cup for the best total times, surprised everyone with its punctual appearance for each test, and had it not been for a breakdown during the distance test it would have

finished higher up than fourth in general classification.

The year 1912 ended in a highly satisfactory manner for the French seaplane constructors. Admittedly the French Navy was not over-enthusiastic about this new device, of which it only ordered a single example, but other nations were already ordering them in more substantial numbers, while air transport 'to order' was becoming a reality with the seaplane.

ENTRIES IN THE COMPETITION FOR RIVER AND COLONIAL SEAPLANES, TAMISE SEPTEMBER 7–16 1912

1	Frank Barra (replaced by Paulhan)	Paulin-Curtiss biplane	Curtiss V8C 75hp
2	Élie Mollien	Paulin-Curtiss biplane	Curtiss V8C 75hp
3	Alfred Lanser	Lanser biplane	Gnome 70hp
4	F. Vershaeve	Jero biplane	Gnome 70hp
5	Charles Weymann	Nieuport monoplane	Gnome 70hp
7	Eugène Renaux	Maurice Faman biplane	Renault 70hp
8	Jean Benoît	Sanchez-Besa biplane	Renault 70hp
9	Émile Ladougne	Sanchez-Besa biplane	Renault 100hp
10	André Beaumont	Donnet-Lévêque biplane	Gnome 80hp
11	Henri Molla	R.E.P. monoplane	Gnome 80hp
12	Louis Gaubert	Astra-Train monplane	Aviatic 100hp
13	Guillaume Busson	L.de Brouckere monoplane	Gnome 100hp
14	Marcel Chambenois (replaced by Chemet)	Borel monoplane	Gnome 80hp
15	Büchow	Aviatic Autovia biplane	Aviatic 100hp

Monaco 1913

The first big meeting in 1913 took place from April 6th to 15th. It started with eliminating tests which consisted of:

– starting the engine on the water without swinging the propeller;

– taking off from the water and climbing to a height of 1,650 feet in less than 30 minutes;

– taking off from the water, levelling out at 330 feet, switching off the engine and touching down on the water;

– showing the ability to be hoisted by a crane;

– being towed by a boat for 100 yards;

– completing 3½ nautical miles entirely on the water.

April 7th was marked by a series of accidents: caught by a gust of wind, the Astra of René Labouret broke a wing on leaving the harbour, and the machine was irretrievably damaged. The three Deperdussins of Louis Janoir, Émile Devienne and Maurice Prévost were damaged as a result of touching down on the water at too high a speed. On April 11th the following qualified: Prévost, whose machine had been repaired, René Moineau and Henri Brégi in their Breguet, Gabriel Espanet and Charles Weymann in a Nieuport, Louis Gaubert in a Maurice-Farman and Jules Fischer in a Henry Farman, who managed the feat of completing all the tests on the last day, his machine also having been seriously damaged before the beginning of the competition.

The next day the flight from Monaco to Beaulieu and San Remo and back to Monaco included three takeoffs, two stops and two tests of seaworthiness over 550 yards. The organizers stuck to the starting time of ten o'clock in spite of a heavy swell. Just as Jules Fischer and Louis Gaubert were taking off, the mistral changed into a gale and the sea opened up troughs 10 or 12 feet deep. Fischer coped well, Gaubert got away with difficulty, and Weymann saw the floats of his Nieuport go under then leap off the crests of the waves before he finally managed to unstick himself from the surface; Espanet was less fortunate and got his Nieuport side on to the swell, then a wave came and twisted the float supports so the pilot returned to the harbour; Brégi skilfully headed his Breguet into the wind and the big biplane literally took off on the spot, while his colleague Moineau had a roller-coaster ride on the waves before finally getting into the air; and Prévost saw his propeller submerged under a mass of water which bent it and forced him to turn back.

When Fischer reached Beaulieu he touched down successfully, but a gust of wind suddenly plunged his wing into the water. The pilot and his mechanic were thrown out of the cockpit, but were quickly recovered from the water. The tail of Weymann's seaplane was torn to pieces by a wave. Towed back into the harbour, all that remained were the floats and the nose of the machine. Brégi and Gaubert wisely decided not to set off again, but Moineau refused to give up. He made for the open sea at a speed which terrified the spectators. They had good reason, because he covered the 27 miles between Beaulieu and San Remo in 15 minutes, an average of 109mph! He managed to touch down, and tried to complete his 550 yards on the water. His machine was battered by the sea for a quarter of an hour, the engine drowned, the propeller broken. He was taken in tow, but the rope broke twice. Moineau and his mechanic climbed onto the central float and were rescued but their seaplane capsized.

Although not one of the competitors completed the course,

Louis Gaubert succeeded in qualifying for the Monaco-San Remo race with his Maurice-Farman (opposite page).

Past and future meet at Monaco: Louis Gaubert's Maurice-Farman presents an unfamiliar vision of the future among the tuna fishing boats .

On April 7th, like all the other Deperdussin pilots, Louis Janoir had an accident. The mounting of the floats was too rigid and caused serious difficulties in touching down.

half of the prizes that had been put up were awarded.

On April 15th the competition for the International Sporting Club prize took place. This was to be decided over 310 miles or, failing that, the distance covered. The circuit for the race, in which only four competitors took part, was polygonal and just over 6 miles round. The Breguet of Henri Brégi quickly took the lead, but stopped with magneto failure after 3½ hours flying and 161 miles. Gaubert flew into a flock of seagulls and bent the copper sheathing protecting the propeller; the resulting vibration caused first the petrol pipes and then the oil pipes to fracture. Each time Gaubert and Aach, his mechanic, calmly repaired them, until the Maurice-Farman had covered 168 miles. The final order was established as follows: first, Louis Gaubert in the Maurice-Farman biplane with 168 miles in 7hrs 40mins; second, Henri Brégi in the Breguet biplane with 161 miles in 3hrs 34mins; third, Gabriel Espanet in the Nieuport monoplane with 118 miles in 3hrs 11mins; fourth, Maurice Prévost in the Deperdussin monoplane with 19 miles.

As a sideshow, Louis Gaubert tried out his flying boat designed by d'Artois. He took off too steeply at the harbour exit and came down from a height of 100 feet, turning over in the process.

A number of conclusions were drawn from the tests. Insufficient knowledge of the sea was noted, on the part of both the constructors and the pilots. However progress had been made as compared to the previous year with the advent of self-starting for the engines, improvements in stability on the water, and the construction of much stronger floats. Breguet's solution was remarkable. The central float, made by Henri Fabre, which could be moved backward or forwards in a few minutes, also had an adjustable rake and an elastic suspension which absorbed the effect of the waves. It was finally noted that the main

difficulties arose from contact with the sea, and more particularly when proceeding over the surface because the machines were then at the mercy of the wind and the waves. In this respect considerable progress still had to be made.

Frank Barra pilots the Astra (far right) in the taxiing tests. The machine did not qualify for the race. The Renault 70hp engine was not sufficiently well protected from the spray.

Henri Brégi's Breguet (right) took part in the race on April 12th 1913.

Maurice Prévost at the controls of his Deperdussin, wearing a life-jacket as is his mechanic standing on the float.

It was in this seaplane that he won the first Schneider Trophy.

The 1913 Schneider Trophy

The first Schneider Trophy took place at the same time as the main Monaco event. As it was an international speed competition with a maximum of only three competitors representing each nation, eliminating rounds were needed for the French competitors. Maurice Prévost, Roland Garros and Gabriel Espanet qualified and were opposed, on April 16th, by Charles Weymann, a pilot of American nationality.

In magnificent weather, Prévost in his Deperdussin and Garros in his Morane-Saulnier dashed off. The first of these covered 2½ miles in less than 7 minutes, while the second broke down. Repaired in an hour and a half, it took off, broke a pushrod, was repaired again and set off in pursuit. Gabriel Espanet in the Nieuport gave up with engine trouble. The battle for the lead was reduced to a duel between Prévost and Weymann, whose machines had the same engine: the double-row radial 160hp Gnome, which was very difficult to adjust correctly. The American pilot lost time on the water but made up for this with a higher average speed, putting in some laps at 69mph. At 93 miles he had a three second lead over Prévost, who touched down on the water 550 yards before the finish line and reached the harbour. He had covered 168 miles in 2hrs 50mins but had not crossed the finish line in flight as stipulated by the regulations. After 45 minutes of agitated discussion, he gave way, and his time was adjusted to 3hrs 48mins. He nearly lost the Trophy as a result, but Weymann was forced to stop after

149 miles because of a seized piston and did not succeed in getting away again.

The Jacques Schneider Trophy therefore went to France.

The d'Artois was so badly designed that it sank during a test which was not part of the competition, injuring its pilot, Louis Gaubert.

The Borel seaplane arriving at Deauville after a flight of three hours forty-seven minutes.

Paul Rugère's Bathiat-Sanchez taking off from the Pecq park, August 24th 1913. This machine was the first to retire from the race.

The Paris-Deauville Race

The second event of 1913 was the Paris-Deauville race and marine aircraft competition. The former took place on August 24th. Nine pilots took off from the Seine on the edge of the Pecq park, watched by 50,000 spectators, in an event that soon turned into total chaos. Charles Weymann in his Nieuport decided to fly at very low altitude and hit a tree at Saint-Pierre-de-Vauvray, splashed down disastrously, then took the wings off the monoplane with the aid of his mechanic, arriving the next morning at Deauville after taxiing on the water for a record distance. Adrien Levasseur at least chose the right altitude, but came down around midday at Honfleur with magneto trouble and finally arrived at 4pm. The last straw was that he was later disqualified because he was not recognized by the race officials at Mousseaux. Louis Janoir in his Deperdussin suffered numerous breakdowns which forced him to come down on the water five times, and he eventually reached Deauville 10 minutes outside the specified time. Maurice Prévost retired. François Molla on his Lévêque did not get away until 10.30am, after remedying the flow in his fuel system. Not bothering about the race, he stopped at Vernon for lunch; on taking off again, he encountered gusts of wind whistling through the Seine valley and put down again at Avilleboeuf, finally reaching Deauville at 5.46pm. Imagine his astonishment when he heard that he had come second in the race! Georges Chemet took off without difficulty from the Pecq park at 9.07am and in spite of having only a modest 80hp engine successfully braved the elements; after flying for 3hrs 47mins he reached the beach at Deauville to win the race, at an average of less than 56mph. After several fruitless attempts to get away and after returning to the starting line several times, Paul Rugère gave up at Vernon. Olivier de Montalent was caught up in violent turbulence just before Rouen; the pilot and his mechanic, Métivier, were thrown out and went crashing to the ground, while their Breguet came down like a falling leaf. This fatal accident cast a shadow over the race. Divetain on the Borel Aéroyacht damaged the hull when touching down at Elbeuf. He waited until night to go on to Deauville.

Curiously, while most of the machines had already proved themselves at Monaco, only two qualified as finishers in the race, and for the first time a seaplane with a hull – a flying boat – showed up to advantage. The triumph of the Borel Hydravion was one for simplicity and lightness of construction, also for the Gnome 80hp engine which made up for its lack of power with remarkable reliability. The race also showed that flying over inland areas was not always a simple matter, since even in fine weather dangerous turbulence could be lying in wait.

ENTRIES FOR THE PARIS-DEAUVILLE RACE, AUGUST 24 1913

1	Charles Weymann	Nieuport monoplane	Gnome 160hp	Nieuport floats
2	Adrien Levasseur	Nieuport monoplane	Gnome 110hp	Nieuport floats
3	Louis Janoir	Deperdussin monoplane	Gnome 160hp	Tellier floats
4	Maurice Prévost	Deperdussin monoplane	Gnome 160hp	Tellier floats
5	Émile Devienne	Deperdussin monoplane	Gnome 80hp	Tellier floats
6	François Molla	Lévêque biplane	Gnome 80hp	Denhaut hull
7	Georges Chemet	Borel Hydravion monoplane	Gnome 80hp	Borel floats
8	Paul Rugère	Bathiat-Sanchez biplane	Gnome 160hp	Bathiat-Sanchez floats
9	Olivier de Montalent	Breguet H-U3 biplane	Salmson 130hp	Fabre and Tellier floats
10	Pierre Divetain	Borel Aéroyacht biplane	Anzani 80hp	Denhaut hull

Marine Aircraft Competition Deauville 1913

The aim of the Marine Aircraft Competition was to select two types of machine for use by the French Navy: 'coastal' aircraft and 'shipboard' aircraft. The latter were intended to be carried on board, and had to demonstrate the ability to take off using wheels in 115 feet and have folding wings.

Thirteen competitors presented themselves for the eliminating trials. Seaworthiness as well as suitability for reconnaissance missions were scrupulously tested. The figures relating to takeoff distance, taxiing and climbing speeds as well as manoeuvrability were precisely recorded.

The days were not lacking in incident. The Borel Aéroyacht sank on arriving from Elbeuf, but once the damage to the hull had been repaired, Pierre Divetain completed the demonstrations as a non-competitor.

Also on August 25th, Félix Bosano took out his Dussot monoplane for the first time. The machine bounced on the sea, lifted out of the water, reared up, gained a little height, then went into a nose dive and sank. The slightly injured pilot was quickly rescued.

The next day the Caudron Type K turned over. Gaston

Caudron rescued his brother and Alessandro Anzani, the builder of the engine. They both clung to the floats of the rescue aircraft as it taxied along – the first rescue at sea by a seaplane.

The qualifying tests soon became monotonous: too many of the takeoffs were painfully difficult, and after two days the interminable succession of participants no longer attracted the public. The two Farmans were immobilized because their floats, which had wrongly located steps, prevented takeoff. On August 26th Eugène Renaux fitted the flat-bottomed floats which he had already used at Monaco. Two days later Gaubert received similar items from the British Navy. Gaston Caudron decided that he for his part would only participate in the special test for shipboard aircraft, and found himself on his own. He took off in less than 115 feet from the launching ramp, and took the 6,000 franc prize.

Eight competitors were selected to take part in the final trials, which took place from August 29th onwards. Although before the competition observers had been worried about the severity of the requirements, on the day itself Molla's Lévêque took the prize for the best average over 250 nautical miles with a speed of 53.18mph, including one stop. Moineau's Breguet won the prize for speed over 100 nautical miles with 62.4mph. A failure of the cooling system prevented it from going any further than 100 miles, but it was more than 6mph faster than Georges Chemet's Borel which was placed second.

On August 30th the endurance test showed the Maurice-Farmans to best advantage: Eugène Renaux covered 300 nautical miles in 6hrs 40mins before stopping when a connecting rod came through the sump. Louis Gaubert completed 250 nautical miles in 5hrs 36mins. Placed equal first, they shared the 54,000 franc prize for covering at least 250 nautical miles.

On the same day Prévost in his Deperdussin was 2½ minutes

Georges Chemet shouts for joy on hearing the news of his victory in the Paris-Deauville race, while his mechanic Toufflet has not yet realized what has happened.
Note the inscription "Hydravion" (seaplane) on the cowling and also the sheathing on the propeller blade, an essential protection against the spray.

The Breguet HU-3 of René Moineau is brought into position by the mechanics.
Its characteristic feature was that the two wings were separate from the fuselage

The Salmson engine mounted in the fuselage of the Breguet HU-3 gave 200hp, but its weight offset the gain in power.
This frontal view shows how the central float is separate from the lower wings and the fuselage.

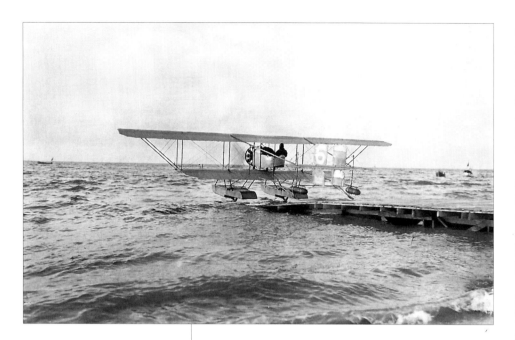

Gaston Caudron's Caudron takes off from the temporary slipway.

The pilot won the test for 'shipboard' aircraft, for which he was the sole entrant. This machine was also the only amphibian in the Deauville competition.

conclusive, because the constructors did not produce any machines that were very different from those at Monaco. Even so, it is noticeable that the accidents were a result either of incorrect trim as in the case of the Dussot, or of an excessively rigid frame as with the Nieuport and Deperdussin machines. Although provided with rubber shock absorbers, they could not in fact be relied on for regular service at sea, though adequate for use at meetings.

The main innovation concerned the engines, which were much more powerful than at Monaco. The non-rotary engines turned out to be the only ones capable of standing up to long distances. Reinforcement of the propeller blades was an absolute requirement. Various opinions were held on the subject of floats, but it was certain that the buoyancy of the tail floats was insufficient to give the required stability.

After a scrupulous analysis the French Navy finally chose the Breguet H-U3 with the Salmson engine, ordering two examples, but the Monaco results must have weighed more heavily in this choice than the Deauville results.

The last two big competitions of 1913 took place at San Sebastian from September 20th to 27th and on the Italian lakes. The first was won by Renaux in his Maurice-Farman and the second by Roland Garros with his Morane-Saulnier. This final event was dominated by the German Helmut Hirth, whose Albatros showed itself to be greatly superior to all its opponents, although it was disqualified for some obscure reason. It was now up to France to respond to progress made elsewhere in Europe as well as in America.

ahead of Moineau at 100 nautical miles, but his achievement was not officially recognized. Levasseur and Janoir retired, and Weymann bent the mountings of his floats and retired. On the last day the sea was rough. Renaux and Gaubert took the 15,000 francs for the takeoff test. Moineau and Chemet were less at home in the waves, while Prévost broke his airframe on a wave; his Deperdussin, barely afloat, was recovered by sailors placed at the organizers' disposal.

The lessons of the Deauville competition were not

ENTRIES FOR THE MARINE AIRCRAFT COMPETITION, DEAUVILLE AUGUST 25-31 1913

1	Eugène Renaux	Maurice-Farman biplane	Renault 120hp	Tellier-Farman floats
2	Louis Gaubert	Maurice-Farman biplane	Salmson 120hp	Tellier-Farman floats
3	Charles Weymann	Nieuport monoplane	Gnome 160hp	Nieuport floats
4	Adrien Levasseur	Nieuport monoplane	Gnome 160hp	Nieuport floats
5	René Caudron	Caudron Type K biplane	Anzani 100hp	Fabre floats
6	Gaston Caudron	Caudron biplane	Anzani 200hp	Fabre floats
7	Paul Rugère	Bathiat-Sanchez biplane	Gnome 160hp	Bathiat-Sanchez floats
8	René Moineau	Breguet biplane	Salmson 200hp	Fabre and Tellier floats
9	Henri Brégi	Breguet biplane	Salmson 200hp	Fabre and Tellier floats
10	Louis Janoir	Deperdussin monoplane	Gnome 100hp	Deperdussin floats
11	Maurice Prévost	Deperdussin monoplane	Gnome 200hp	Deperdussin floats
12	Georges Chemet	Borel Hydravion monoplane	Gnome 80hp	Borel floats
13	Félix Bosano	Dussot monoplane	Anzani 100hp	Dussot hull
14	Wladimir de Lambert	Astra biplane	Gnome 160hp	Tellier floats
15	François Molla	Lévêque biplane	Salmson 120hp	Denhaut hull

Roland Garros prepares to start the Gnome 80hp engine of his Morane-Saulnier, while a mechanic swings the propeller.

Eugène Renaux about to take off in a Maurice-Farman.

Monaco 1914

The 1914 season began with the Monaco air rally, which took as its aim the development of tourism by air over both land and sea. Several itineraries with stopovers were offered to the 25 contestants, ending either at Genoa or Marseilles. There a relay was set up to allow either a change of aircraft or the addition of floats in order to make a trip of 130 miles across the sea to Monaco.

On this occasion the rivalry between Hirth and Garros came out in favour of the famous French aviator, who won by covering the route Monaco-Marseilles-Bordeaux-Angers-Buc in 12hrs 14mins.

In so far as the competition was for land-based aircraft rather than genuine seaplanes, its lesson was above all that the fitting of floats to an aircraft is a more complex operation than it may seem. Hirth realized this on April 6th when coming down on the water at Tamaris, where the Albatros capsized. Only Roland Garros in a Morane-Saulnier completed the sea route three times, while Brindejonc des Moulinais in an identical machine, Eugène Renaux in a Maurice-Farman, Verrier in a Henry Farman, and Malard in a Nieuport monoplane managed it once.

The 1914 Schneider Trophy

The great event for seaplanes remained the Schneider Trophy, for which five nations had submitted entries: Germany, France, Great Britain, Switzerland and the USA. The French eliminating round took place on April 8th between Maurice Prévost and Louis Janoir on Deperdussins, Gabriel Espanet and Adrien Levasseur in Nieuports, with Brindejonc and Garros in Morane-Saulniers. Espanet won, followed by Levasseur and Garros.

The sturdiness and reliability of the Albatros with its 150hp Benz engine greatly impressed observers.

An accident at Tamaris prevented the machine from taking part in the Schneider Trophy.

Howard Pixton's Sopwith makes a banked turn above a control boat.

This machine won the 1914 Schneider Trophy, showing itself greatly superior to its French opponents.

On April 20th, in magnificent weather but with a strong wind, Gabriel Espanet appeared on the starting line with Adrien Levasseur behind him, then Howard Pixton in a Sopwith, John Carbery, and Ernest Burri who was representing Switzerland with his F.B.A., an improved version of the Lévêque under a new name, the Franco-British Aviation.

The competition took place over a more or less triangular circuit of less than six miles. Each competitor had to come down at least once during his first lap. The superiority of the Sopwith immediately became clear, as it completed its first circuit in 4mins 27sec as compared with 6mins 17sec for Burri's F.B.A., its closest rival.

Howard Pixton was performing wonders at the controls of the Sopwith, his seaplane achieving remarkable speeds of up to 93mph. After 62 miles of the race he had a lead of more than ten minutes over Gabriel Espanet, then came Adrien Levasseur and Ernest Burri. Gabriel Espanet came down on the 16th lap, his engine having failed with a with a seized piston, likewise Levasseur on the following lap; they returned to the shore and retired. Lord John Carbery exchanged his Morane-Saulnier for Louis Janoir's Deperdussin, but after one lap and numerous bounces on the sea he decided to give up .

Pixton and Burri remained the only runners, but their machines were too different for there to be any real contest between them.

Thus the final order was: first Howard Pixton with 150 nautical miles (173 miles) in 2hrs 13sec, and second Ernest Burri with 150 nautical miles in 3hrs 24mins. The difference in the times was further accentuated by a refuelling stop of 37 minutes.

Once again 100hp engines had won due to their reliability, whereas the 160hp engines with their excessive complexity had not lasted the course.

The conclusion to be drawn from the 1914 Schneider Trophy

was that the two forms of seaplane should be developed on complementary, but separate, lines.

Three years of competitions, meetings and races had not produced any ideal formulae or proved the relative qualities of the flying boat versus the float-plane. However, they did awaken some real interest in these new machines, even if the results had not matched up to the expectations.

The Swiss Ernest Burri in an F.B.A. (right) never thought he would finish second in the 1914 Schneider Trophy, but he was more than an hour behind the winner.

The Sopwith Tabloid (far right) leaving the harbour at Monaco on its way to the starting line.

Howard Pixton on the port float displays typically British nonchalance. Not only did he win the race, but he also established a speed record for seaplanes by covering 186 miles at 90.89mph.

Gabriel Espanet's Nieuport passes overhead.
He retired, let down by his 160hp Gnome engine.

CHAPTER 2

The First World War

THE FIRST WORLD WAR BROKE OUT FOUR YEARS AFTER THE FIRST FLIGHT BY A SEAPLANE. THE MOST OBVIOUS USE FOR SEAPLANES SEEMED TO BE FOR RECONNAISSANCE; IT VERY SOON BECAME CLEAR THAT THEY WERE NOT SUITABLE FOR A COMBAT ROLE. WHEN PEACE RETURNED, THE EXPERIENCE GAINED DURING THE WAR WAS TO PROVIDE THE STARTING POINT FOR A REMARKABLE EXPANSION IN MARINE AVIATION.

An F.B.A. Type H is drawn up a slipway made of planks at Hourtin.

A close-up of the Hispano-Suiza engine and the gun positions of an F.B.A. Type H.

The First World War produced a quite spectacular development in marine aviation. Before 1914 the use of seaplanes had largely been confined to sporting events. By the time of the Armistice in 1918, they had improved greatly in power, safety and all-round ability. They had performed a wide range of tasks: reconnaissance, sea patrols, anti-submarine warfare, torpedoing as well as bombing and pursuing ships, and air sea rescue. In spite of the seaplane's inferior performance in terms of pure speed compared with other kinds of aircraft, its versatility meant that it was highly regarded. The independence in operation of the large flying boats, meanwhile, pressaged their commercial exploitation in the near future on transoceanic routes.

However, marine aviation did not develop to the same extent in all countries.

GERMANY

Marine aviation in Germany had its beginnings in the work of August von Parseval in 1909. This resulted in the production of an amphibian flying boat balanced by two wing-floats and with very high wings, on which were mounted two propellers driven by a Daimler 120hp engine. This seaplane, with an unladen weight of 2,090lb, was much too ambitious for the power outputs of the time. After numerous attempts on the Plauer See in Mecklenburg, the Parseval achieved liftoff under its own power in April 1910.

The German Navy became interested in aviation in 1910, and in August 1911 five pilots were commissioned, one of whom was Lieutenant J.S. Langfeld, who made the first flight by a German seaplane in May 1912. This was the Albatros WD3 (actually a Farman built under licence), fitted with a central float designed by Coulmann.

The first German competition for seaplanes took place at Heiligendamm from August 29th to September 5th; the three best machines, the Aviatik, Albatros WD5 and Ago biplanes, all of which were powered by Argus 100hp engines, took part in a competition at Putzig in the autumn.

In the spring of 1913, the Fliegerstationen (air bases) of Putzig (Danzig), Kiel, Heligoland and Wilhelmshaven were established, but due to lack of resources only the first two were really operational when war was declared. Meanwhile the constructors confronted one another in competitions on Lake Constance. These were won by the Albatros float-monoplane designed by Ernst Heinkel, and they saw some fine performances such as that of Henreich Dahm in the Friedrichshafen amphibious biplane with which he flew to Cologne, Amsterdam, Cuehmen and Hamburg, touching down on rivers and estuaries. The Reichsmarine did not hesitate to get hold of English machines (the Avro and the Sopwith Batboat), American (the Curtiss Flying Boat), then Austrian (the Lohner), in order to study in depth the technical features of the foreign machines.

Yet in spite of all these efforts, lack of manpower and the inadequate performance of the seaplanes made it impossible to put them into service at the beginning of the conflict. The first operational unit was set up at Zeebrugge in December 1914, and was equipped with a mere four Friedrichshafen FF29 float-planes.

Three years later the German Navy had 27 bases spread out over the Baltic, the Black Sea, the Adriatic and the North Sea. By the end of the war it had 673 combat seaplanes and 446 for training and experimental purposes. It also had one of the aces of marine aviation, Friedrich Christiansen.

AUSTRIA-HUNGARY

The Kaiserliche und Königliche Kriegsmarine (Austro-Hungarian Navy) showed interest at an early stage, pilots being trained in France and Great Britain from 1909 onwards. Two years later, an experimental aeronautical centre was set up on the island of Santa Catarina in Pola harbour. In December 1911, orders were sent to

A line-up of Friedrichshafen FF 33Ls of the Seeflugstation Flanders 1 based at Zeebrugge in September 1917.
The FF33 was the most numerous multipurpose seaplane built in Germany during the war.

A crew member detaches a sling from a Friedrichshafen 33S.
This version was used for advanced pilot training.

Captured at Vordingborg in Denmark, this Hansa-Brandenburg W.12 (below left) had a 160hp Mercedes engine.

The Dornier CS1 taking off from Lake Constance in the summer of 1918.
Intended to replace the heavy-duty Brandenburg fighters, it could fly at 112mph. However, it did not go into service before the Armistice.

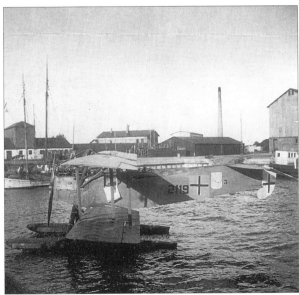

An improved derivative of the
F.B.A. acquired before the war
by the Austro-Hungarian Navy,
the Lohner Type Te was a multipurpose flying boat,
photographed here at Santa
Catarina in April 1916.
L65 had a 160hp Daimler engine.

The Brandenburg W.13 was a
heavy three-seater aircraft
fitted with a 345hp
Daimler engine.

40

three Austrian constructors, Mickl, Warchalowski and Lohner and – because of the problems encountered in the design of seaplanes – to foreign firms as well; officers sent to France recommended the purchase of three Donnet-Lévêques, which were to be known as Lévêques, then F.B.A.s. Orders for two Paulhan-Curtiss Type Fs and a Sanchez-Besa followed.

Tried out in France in October 1912, the F.B.A. Type Cs were used in the blockade operations on the coast of Montenegro, and undertook reconnaissance missions for the Austrian torpedo boats. Once the blockade was in place, they covered the 300 miles to Pola under their own power, and were used for training aircrews there.

The Mickl, in spite of being underpowered with only 35hp, took Rudolf Graf von Montecuccoli on a flight, and he became the first admiral to have flown in a seaplane.

The engineers Karl Paulal and Leopold Bauer, who worked for Lohner, were decisively influenced by the F.B.A.s. They brought out the 1913 type Lohner fitted with a Gnome 100hp engine, and its flying qualities turned out to be superior to those of the F.B.A., the additional wing area counting for much in this result. Only one example was built but this flying boat sired a whole line of Lohners and Brandenburgs.

By the time the First World War was declared, the Austro-Hungarian Navy had 22 machines, a third of which were of foreign origin. Twelve of them were used for training.

The combat aircraft took part in battle; from August 15th 1914 a Lohner Type M (E-18) bombed Krstac on the Albanian coast. In spite of the entry of Italy into the war, the Austro-Hungarian force did not reach the spectacular proportions of those of the other belligerents. Altogether more than 600 seaplanes and flying boats were delivered between 1914 and 1918, mainly by the German Heinkel company under the names Hansa-Brandenburg, Lohner and Phönix.

At the time of the Armistice, the Austrian Navy had 257 machines, of which 150 were genuinely operational, although with some difficulty since there were only about 50 pilots. Even so, due to judicious use of its resources the Austrian Imperial Navy could pride itself on having amongst them Gottfried Banfield, one of the rare fighter aces who had gained his victories in a seaplane.

FRANCE

Even though the French Navy had shown some interest in aviation in 1910 by qualifying five sailors as pilots that summer, the acquisition of aircraft was a very slow process. Certainly there were some visionaries who wanted to forge ahead and defined

Lohner Type Te no. L 78 was captured by the Italians on May 27th 1915, with its floats removed.

It was immediately copied by Macchi as their L.1, the only modification being the fitting of a 150hp Isotta-Fraschini engine.

The Lévy-Le Pen HB2 designed by Blanchard and Le Pen was used as a convoy escort.

It was the first French seaplane capable of carrying 180lb bombs specially designed for attacking submarines.

The Tellier Sunbeam, used for reconnaissance over open sea, was characterized by the two horizontal spars joining the wings to the top of the tail fin.

It is doing a good speed through the water, hence all the spray around the hull.

about ten minutes in the Bay of Fréjus, then was dismantled in order to be hoisted on board the cruiser *Foudre*. The next day it made a flight of 22 minutes at 300 feet with one passenger and a load of nearly 500lb. Colliex landed on the water, filled up with fuel, and took off again with the *Foudre*'s Lieutenant Cayla, but had to interrupt his flight after 33 minutes instead of the specified time, because condensation from the fog was preventing the carburettor from functioning properly. On July 29th, a Nieuport with a 100hp Gnome piloted by Sub-Lieutenant Delage made a series of surveillance flights from the cruiser; it flew to and fro for three hours with two passengers.

Sub-Lieutenant Fournier also participated successfully in the manoeuvres at the controls of a Henry Farman; the H.F. was donated to the Navy by the "French people of the Principality of Monaco" following its victory in the competition. The Canard Voisin was destroyed in August, but the Navy ordered two Nieuports, a Breguet H-U3 and a Maurice-Farman, to which were added another Voisin and a Caudron. Seven seaplanes made up the total strength of the Navy's air force, based at Fréjus. In May 1913 a Nieuport carried on the *Foudre* foiled an enemy attack during major naval manoeuvres.

This success led to the ordering of five new Nieuport seaplanes. It was with machines of this type that three pilots flew from Fréjus to Nice and back in December 1913, while two others flew from Fréjus to Calvi then to Ajaccio on March 13th 1914. This trip of 155 miles was completed in three hours, with a refuelling stop on the Îles Sanguinaires. The Canard Voisin failed in its attempt to accompany them.

These flights in a group anticipated the creation of flights of aircraft, but before that could be done it was necessary to provide

two types of mission: surveillance of the areas around the ports would go to 'coastal seaplanes' and reconnaissance for the benefit of fleets or squadrons would be allocated to machines attached to the ships, 'ship-borne seaplanes'. Their proposals fell largely on deaf ears.

Paul Painlevé, commenting on the military budget, noted that "the efforts that have been made to provide our navy with an aerial fleet are very modest". As for the Delcassé report, which envisaged the creation of seven permanent aviation centres, it did not receive any support.

The first seaplane delivered to the French Navy was a Canard-type Voisin. On June 12th 1912, piloted by Colliex, it flew for

To protect its flying boats based at Dunkirk, the French Navy received some Sopwith Babies, military derivatives of the machine which won the Schneider Trophy.
Their range was, however, insufficient to offer any real threat to the German aircraft

a considerable increase in numbers. In spite of the unquestionable commitment of the constructors, who had produced as many as 146 seaplanes in 1913, the Navy only owned 11 of them. By adding up the number of machines delivered to other countries, it can be seen that twice as many French aircraft were flying outside France.

The big naval manoeuvres in May 1914 involved four Nieuports from Bizerta, two Voisins, two Breguets and a Nieuport based at Fréjus, plus a Caudron and a Voisin operating from the *Foudre*. On May 8th René Caudron took off from the ship using a platform about 30 feet long, thus demonstrating his aircraft's abilities, but it was a very risky operation, and on June 9th his machine fell into the sea when trying to repeat the exploit.

The 1914 manoeuvres, which saw about 100 flying hours clocked up, at the cost of the loss of two machines, showed that seaplanes could successfully take on surveillance missions, and even locate a submerged submarine given favourable conditions.

Since planning seems to have been a matter of supreme indifference to the French Navy, it only had nine flyers and 13 seaplanes, of which only eight were operational, when war was declared in 1914.

The increase in strength remained painfully slow, for the importance of marine aviation had not really been recognized. The surveillance missions carried out from Dunkirk and the defensive sorties made over the Adriatic did not justify any great effort or expenditure.

It was improvements in the machines and the submarine menace that changed the whole picture. While the milestone of 100 seaplanes was not reached until the summer of 1916, the number of machines in service increased to 691 by December 31st 1917 and to 1,264 by the time of the Armistice, of which 870 were operational, spread over 32 naval aviation centres and 21 combat stations.

An F.B.A. Type C showing the speed of rotation of the propeller with direct drive from the engine.
The F.B.A. in all its versions was the flying boat built in the largest numbers during the Great War, and also the most frequently copied.

During the last two years of the war the Short 184 took on the role of the British forces' multi-purpose seaplane.
On board here are two R.A.F. officers.

The Short S.38 undergoing catapult launching tests from *H.M.S. Hibernia* in May 1912.

GREAT BRITAIN

Naval matters have always been of great importance for Great Britain, so it is not surprising that this country paid particular attention to marine aviation as soon as it reached a stage where military uses could be envisaged.

The beginnings of seaplanes in Britain remain obscure. Oscar T. Gnosspelius claimed the honour of being the first to take off from the water, in July 1911, in a machine fitted with Blériot XI wings and two floats. But most historians contest this. Commander Oliver Schwann, having tested over a long period at least seven types of float on the Avro D biplane, took off for a few yards on November 18th, but having had no previous experience of flying he caused the machine to break up when alighting on the water again.

In the end it was a Curtiss built under licence by Avro and fitted with Lakes floats designed in England that made the first 'complete' flight by a seaplane on November 25th 1911.

The Admiralty initially acquired four aircraft of different types, all built by Short. The S.38, which was an imported Sommer biplane with a Gnome 50hp pusher engine and fitted with floats, took off from a platform mounted on *H.M.S. Africa* piloted by Lieutenant Commander Salmson on January 10th 1912. The ship was at anchor. Lightened and fitted with a Gnome 70hp engine, the same machine, again piloted by Salmson, took off from the ramp mounted on *H.M.S. Hibernia* steaming at 10 knots in Weymouth Bay on May 12th 1912 during naval manoeuvres. The future of naval aviation, and more particularly of seaplanes, seemed assured – so much so that purchases followed one another in quick succession.

In November 1911 the Admiralty had four machines, of which only one had been converted into a seaplane. In February 1912 the Royal Navy ordered nine seaplanes, six machines capable of being fitted with floats, and just four land-based aircraft. Whereas five French manufacturers supplied their products, Short was the only British firm chosen. Since the conversion of a seaplane into a land-based aircraft, or vice versa, did not present a problem, the classification of the machines was just a rough guide.

The Admiralty wanted to make the seaplane into a weapon. In December 1913 it experimented with the effect of the blast from small explosive charges on a Maurice-Farman S.7 flying at an altitude of between 300 and 1,000 feet. Since the machine did not suffer any damage, the bombing trials were able to go ahead. Another example was used about this time for firing at aerial targets, which were in fact ducks! Two of these unfortunate birds were hit by the bullets.

In a more serious vein, two seaplanes with pusher engines, the Sopwith and the Gun-carrying Short (S.81), undertook numerous firing tests with machine guns, from May 1914 in the first case and from September in the second case. They demonstrated a defensive ability to be reckoned with.

On the other hand all efforts to adapt torpedoes to suit the Sopwith Special, conceived particularly for this purpose, turned out to be in vain. Eventually Lieutenant Commander Longmore in the Short Admiralty 81 launched a 14in torpedo, but this success was not to be repeated.

The last type of mission allocated to seaplanes was keeping watch over naval squadrons. However, keeping in touch with one's charges required a considerable development in wireless equipment. During naval manoeuvres in May 1912, a Short S.41 Tractor succeeded in transmitting messages over a distance estimated at between 4 and 5½ miles. But this was still inadequate for obtaining usable results in operational conditions.

When war was declared, the Royal Navy had 31 seaplanes

and 40 land-based aircraft, many of which could be fitted with floats. They were stationed at four bases: Calshot, Cromarty, Felixstowe and Great Yarmouth.

The R.N.A.S. (Royal Naval Air Service) was made responsible for the defence of the kingdom's airspace, for the anti-submarine campaign and for the interception of Zeppelins over the North Sea. The multiplication of the number of bases due to the immense size of the Empire meant that by April 1st 1918, when the R.N.A.S. and the R.F.C. (Royal Flying Corps) combined to form the R.A.F. (Royal Air Force), the Admiralty had 126 air stations and 2,949 aircraft (both landplanes and seaplanes).

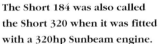

The Short 184 was also called the Short 320 when it was fitted with a 320hp Sunbeam engine. The pilot of N1397 sat in the rear seat.

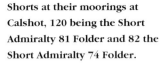

Shorts at their moorings at Calshot, 120 being the Short Admiralty 81 Folder and 82 the Short Admiralty 74 Folder.

GREECE

When the first Balkan war broke out in October 1912, the Greek Army had two Nieuports and three Farmans. Also in October, the Greek Navy had an Astra C.M. seaplane delivered, which was sent to the island of Lemnos, piloted by Guinard.

However, the first seaplane to take part in a military operation was a Maurice-Farman with a 100hp Renault engine fitted with floats. On December 19th 1912, Lieutenant Michael Montoussis accompanied by Sub-Lieutenant Moraïtinis was given the task of reconnoitring the Dardanelles operating from Lemnos. He successfully overflew his objective, and replied to the shots that he attracted by dropping four small home-made bombs on a Turkish lighthouse by hand. Most importantly he was able to give the position of the enemy fleet, over which he circled several times before returning to Lemnos.

Before he could get that far, Lieutenant Montoussis had to bring the Maurice-Farman down in a glide two miles from the island of Imbros, from where the destroyer *Belos* then towed it to rejoin the Greek fleet at Mondras.

In March 1914, the Greek Navy ordered six Sopwith Gunbuses, but the entry of Britain into the war prevented their delivery. The air arm of the Royal Greek Navy came into being in May 1917; it had one Sopwith Baby and one Henry Farman fitted with floats.

ITALY

The first flight of a seaplane in Italy was achieved by Guidoni at the controls of a Henry Farman with floats on November 5th 1910. The first Italian seaplane was designed in 1911 by Lieutenant Caldera, who made demonstration flights over Venice with passengers on board.

The Regia Marina (Italian Navy) was interested in the use of seaplanes as an air arm as early as August 1912. It ordered a Paulhan-Curtiss and sent several officers to the school Louis Paulhan had opened at Juan-les-Pins. Subsequently the Regia Marina bought a Blériot XI-2 seaplane, two Breguet G.3s and four Borels in France, and four Albatros WDDs in Germany, while eight Curtiss Flying Boats were built under licence.

The Macchi M.7 powered by a 250hp Isotta-Fraschini engine was so successful that it was immediately ordered by the Italian Navy.

When Italy entered the war on May 24th 1915, the force was distributed as follows: at Venice seven seaplanes (one Curtiss, two Breguets, four Albatros); at Porto Corsini four Borels; at Pesaro and at Brindisi two Curtisses, giving a total of 15 machines. Compared with the Austrians, who were much better equipped, this was very inadequate, and from May 28th six French seaplanes (F.B.A.s with 80hp Gnomes) began to arrive in Venice, soon reinforced by F.B.A. Type Cs, then four Nieuports were sent to Brindisi during September 1915.

The seaplane industry was to develop in Italy as a result of a curious event. Two days after the beginning of hostilities, a Lohner L.40 was captured intact. Analyzed by Macchi, it was then copied and fitted with an Isotta-Fraschini 150hp engine. Rather mischievously called the L.1, 139 of them were built by Macchi. It was the first in a long line of flying boats.

In spite of the qualities of the Macchi, the Regia Marina chose mainly F.B.A.s, which in various versions totalled 982 examples made by five different manufacturers; this number is equal to all the other Italian seaplanes delivered up to the end of the war. On November 11th 1918 the force was divided into five *squadriglie di* *caccia* (fighter squadrons) and 31 *squadriglie di ricognizione* (reconnaissance squadrons).

The Italian Navy had one fighter ace, Sub-Lieutenant Orazio Pierozzi, who recorded most of his seven combat victories with a Macchi M.5.

The Macchi L.1 was an exact copy of the Lohner Type Te. Only the engine was changed.

Lieutenant Kameko in his Maurice-Farman (Renault 70hp engine) touches down after flying from Yokosuka to Hayama, where the Japanese Emperor is about to congratulate him.

JAPAN

The first demonstration of a seaplane in Japan was given at Yokohama on May 11th 1912 by a Curtiss piloted by an American. The Japanese Navy set up an Aeronautical Research Committee, which sent officers to France and the United States. They gave orders to Curtiss and Maurice-Farman before returning to Japan to take part in naval manoeuvres watched by the Emperor of Japan, Taisho Tenno, on November 12th 1912, 10 days after Lieutenants Yozo Kaneko in an M.F. and Sankichi Kono in a Curtiss had made their first flights from the base at Oppama.

In July 1913, Chikuhei Nakajima produced an improved version of the Farman float-plane, the first machine that the Japanese regarded as a local product destined for their navy. They also tested a Deperdussin similar to the winner of the Schneider Trophy, but it did not meet their needs.

Honouring their obligations under the Anglo-Japanese alliance, the Japanese declared war on Germany. The *Wakamiya Maru*, with three M.F.s on board, arrived in Kiaoshu Bay on September 1st 1914. That same day the seaplanes carried out their first combat mission in aerial warfare. Five days later, the aircraft flew over the German warships and confirmed the absence of the cruiser *Emden*.

The operations which followed were the subject of some controversy: the Japanese claimed that they had sunk a minesweeper with 'bombs' made from ordinary shells, whereas the Germans stated that they had scuttled their three ships. The achievement claimed by the Japanese seems all the more improbable because the Farmans were obliged to fly at an altitude of at least 6,500 feet to avoid enemy fire.

The only aircraft the Germans had at their disposal, a Taube piloted by Lieutenant Günter Pluschow, was pursued on October 13th by all the available Japanese aircraft and seaplanes, but the pilot managed to hide in a thick layer of cloud.

On March 6th 1915 occurred the first loss of an aircrew, in a Farman. On April 1st 1916 the Aeronaval Corps of Yokosuka replaced the Aeronautical Research Committee.

The same year Nakajima and Magoshi produced the first Japanese seaplane, the Type Ho Yokosho, of which four were made; it was followed by the smaller Ho Otsu and then the series production Type Ro-Ko of 1917, of which 218 were produced.

The Imperial Navy also bought machines abroad, and in 1917 bought its first fighter seaplane, a Sopwith Tabloid, as well as some Short 184s and 320s for reconnaissance and torpedo warfare, and even a 200hp Tellier.

RUSSIA

In February 1912, the Imperial Russian Navy ordered about 10 Canard Voisin seaplanes, which were in fact amphibious. In March, the commander of the Black Sea Fleet set up an aeronautical section which was attached to the liaison services, based at Sebastopol. In May, Rugère supervised the delivery of the first two aircraft. After giving a few lessons to Lieutenant Stakowsky, he took advantage of the fact that the Black Sea Fleet was less than 10 miles away to take two passengers for a flight among the ships, followed by his talented pupil. Some Curtiss Triad seaplanes were soon added to the Voisins to complete the Imperial Russian force.

During the summer of 1912, Igor Sikorsky, who was then only 23, was recruited as an engineer in the aeronautical section of the Baltic Fleet. His task was to provide solutions to problems encountered by the aerial reconnaissance branch. The main difficulty was the engines' lack of reliability, but coming down on the water meant a lesser risk for offshore missions, both for the aircrews and for the machines. Sikorsky was to produce a whole series of seaplanes while with the R-BVZ. The S-5A with two floats made its first flight in December 1912 in St Petersburg harbour. The Imperial Navy turned it down because it was underpowered. A second example fitted with a single float and a more powerful engine was accepted for the Baltic Fleet in the spring of 1913. The only seaplane produced in a small production run by Sikorsky was the S-10 Gidro, which made its first flight during the summer of 1913; about 16 examples were built between then and 1915. They were to be used for training at the Revel base in the Gulf of Finland, or at the Libau base on the island of Ezel.

The most famous of the Russian seaplanes was the *Ilya Mourometz*. Designed as a land-based aircraft, it was acquired by the Baltic Fleet to try out as a possible reconnaissance machine. The first four-engined seaplane in history, it was fitted with wooden floats with rubber springs to absorb shocks on taking off and touching down on the water. The test flights carried out at the Libau base were very promising, but the machine was intentionally destroyed by its aircrew on the first day of the war, for fear that it would fall into the hands of the Germans.

Dimitri P. Grigorovich was not nearly as well known as Sikorsky. Taken on in 1913 by the workshops of Shchetinin and Shcherbakov, who made copies of the Nieuport IV and Farman F.16, he discovered his gifts as a designer of seaplanes by accident. D.N. Alexandrov, the then owner of a Donnet-Lévêque, was looking for someone to repair his machine, which had just suffered an accident. Grigorovich offered his services for one fifteenth of the amount demanded by R-BVZ and Lebed; what is more he did not stop at rebuilding the machine, he also improved it by cutting down the fuselage, fitting wings with a new profile and reducing the step in the hull. The M.1 (M standing for *Morskoi*, navy) flew for the first time in the autumn of 1913 and showed improved flying qualities.

The M.2, which followed at the beginning of 1914, was the first flying boat designed and built in Russia, although there was no denying its close affinity with François Denhaut's machines. It was built in a small production run for the Baltic Fleet.

A small single-seater fighter, the Grigorovich M.11 came too late to provide opposition for the German seaplanes and did not go into series production.

The Grigorovich M.5 was also derived from the F.B.A. used in Russia.

The M.5 was this manufacturer's great success. He later offered his services to the Bolsheviks.

A Curtiss HS-2L about to be hauled ashore. Capable of 84mph thanks to its 360hp Liberty 12 engine, it was the most numerous American reconnaissance aircraft of its day with 117 examples built, of which only 15 took part in the war in France.

A view of the entire strength of seaplanes in service with the U.S. Navy in 1914: Curtis Es and Fs based at Pensacola in Florida.

UNITED STATES OF AMERICA

Although Curtiss's name rightly occupies pride of place in the history of marine aviation in the United States, other names do come up. First and foremost was Wright, his constant rival, from whom the U.S. Navy ordered a machine when making its first seaplane purchases, at the same time as two Curtiss Model Es. Other names were to become famous, such as Loughead (Lockheed) or Glenn Martin. Some were to leave a faint trace, such as Benoist who started the first regular service in Florida between St Petersburg and Tampa. From January 1st to March 31st 1914, two machines carried 1,204 passengers, covering the 18 miles in about 20 minutes. The service was suspended in April because of insufficient demand.

While the E and F Models were being sold all over the world, Curtiss took up a new challenge: the Atlantic crossing, for which *The Daily Mail* was offering a prize. Financed by R. Wanamaker, the Model H benefited from the experience of two Britons, B. Douglas Thorn who designed the wings, and John C. Porte who had the task of piloting the machine with Lieutenant John Towers of the U.S. Navy.

Baptized *America* in June 1914, the flying boat was hastily fitted with an additional engine so that it could take off with the large amount of fuel needed. Having completed its first flight on June 22nd, it was ready to make the attempt, but war was declared and Porte therefore was forced to return to Britain. Using his influence, he saw to it that the R.N.A.S. ordered the first two examples of the Model H.4 Small America. These were followed by 54 machines delivered by Curtiss and eight others built in Britain, which were the ancestors of a whole line of flying boats used for patrol work.

The U.S. Navy ordered its first 27 aircraft, all seaplanes or convertible to seaplanes. Twenty came from Curtiss, four from Burgess and three from Wright. The Curtiss AB-3 (Model F) undertook the first operational mission by an American aircraft, on April 25th 1914, when Lieutenant Bellinger flew over Veracruz to observe any Mexican troop movements, then to check whether there were any mines in the harbour entrance. He did not meet any opposition.

During the first years of the Great War, the Americans felt protected by their distance from the field of battle. When they eventually declared war on Germany on April 6th 1917, the U.S.Navy had 54 machines — nearly all seaplanes — but not one of them was operational, as they were used solely for the training of the 48 qualified pilots.

Whereas the Air Corps used exclusively foreign equipment, the Navy succeeded in integrating indigenous products with those of the countries where its men were deployed.

When the war was over, it had 1,865 seaplanes, 329 of which saw active service in Europe; 280 were patrol aircraft designed by Curtiss, 26 of which were for training; some were French machines, 22 Macchi and Sopwith fighters and one a Paul Schmitt torpedo aircraft.

The Curtiss H.12 prototype code-numbered A152 benefited from the work of John C. Porte on large hulls.
Fitted with 250hp Rolls Royce engines, it was capable of up to 110mph.

SHIPBOARD SEAPLANES

When war was declared, the Nieuport flight was the only French unit specifically intended for naval aviation. On August 2nd it only had three examples of the 80hp monoplane with floats, which returned to Nice. Five machines were taken to satisfy an order from Turkey. The flight reached Bizerta on September 1st, and two seaplanes were ferried to Antivari by the *Foudre* to keep Cattaro under surveillance. This detachment was soon lost, as was a second, largely because these operations were carried out without any preparation. These losses raised serious doubts about the value of naval aviation.

However on December 1st the flight, consisting of five aircraft, was deployed at Port Said to serve under the orders of the British Army, entrusted with the task of protecting the Suez Canal from the Turks.

The main function of the flight was to provide an account of the enemy's movements, and the French pilot was accompanied on these scout missions by an English observer with an excellent knowledge of the area. Their secondary tasks involved attacking enemy encampments with a carbine and 'bombing' railways with derisory explosive devices thrown by hand, or observing the movements of shipping at sea.

The unit operated from Smyrna to Jedda, one section being sent to the Dardanelles for the duration of the campaign. It was possible to cover these enormous distances by using British warships or cargo ships for refuelling. Taking off from the sea, the Nieuports undertook raids more than 60 miles inland, both in the desert and in areas where the mountains rose to over 6,000 feet.

There were many acts of heroism: a pilot and his observer returned to their lines on foot one day with a prisoner, having abandoned their aircraft in the middle of the desert; the next day mechanics were put down on the spot to collect an engine and any useful parts as there was a desperate shortage of spares. Fortunately the flight received some new aircraft in May 1915, at the end of its Dardanelles mission.

It was during this deployment that a crew managed to remove the floats in the record time of one hour, to help the Nieuports to gain altitude more rapidly to escape enemy fire. Because of the lack of engine reliability, extended flights by seaplanes over land represented a serious risk. but the flight had

A Nieuport seaplane being launched from the *Campinas*. It belonged to the Port Said flight, which defended British interests in the Middle East

The Fairey Type 127 N9 underwent a series of catapult launching tests before being adopted by the R.A.F.
Held here on a launching ramp, this machine was the prototype of the Fairey IIIA, which appeared at the end of the War.

No. 841 *Wölfchen* (wolf cub) was the aircraft carried by the German raider *Wolf* on its destructive cruise across three oceans from November 1916 to February 1918.
It is a Friedrichshafen FF33E.

seasoned pilots, capable of touching down gently, even on the verge of stalling and with the engine switched off.

On April 18th 1916 the Nieuport flight left Port Said with eight aircraft, four of which had seen 11 months of service and the other four 18 months. Only half of the flying personnel were left, but the sacrifice of these men had given the British time to organize their aerial forces in Egypt.

For its part, the Nieuport with an engine of only 100hp had shown exceptional qualities in the air and on the water, coping equally well with sandstorms, powerful currents and torrid heat, which proved that seaplanes could operate in to extreme conditions.

The combatants used aircraft carried on ships and even on submarines. The most notorious tour of duty was that of the Friedrichshafen FF33E *Wölfchen*, which, operated from *S.M.S. Wolf*. Over a period of 15 months, it took part in the destruction or the capture of 28 ships in the South Atlantic, the Indian Ocean and the Pacific.

The British perfected techniques of catapult-launching, which could only be used with seaplanes that could be picked up again later from the sea.

This Gotha WD 7 no. 119 was put on display at Dunkirk as spoils of war.

On April 4th 1916, this Gotha WD 7 no. 119 was forced to touch down.
When the crew saw a French vessel arriving, they set the seaplane on fire.

TORPEDO-CARRYING SEAPLANES

At a very early stage, strategists had conceived the idea of using seaplanes for launching torpedoes, but it soon became clear that the development of special aircraft for this purpose was more difficult than expected. The British took up the challenge first.

Ordered in July 1914, the Short 184 arrived at Felixstowe in April 1915. It was a braced wing biplane fitted with a 225hp Sunbeam engine and two wooden floats between which was carried a 14in torpedo weighing nearly 800lb. The tests of the two first prototypes seemed so encouraging that two 184s were allocated to the seaplane-carrier *Ben-my-Chree*, which arrived in the vicinity of the Dardanelles on June 12th. Their mission was to attack the battleship *Goeben* and the cruiser *Breslau*, assigned to the Turkish Navy under the names *Yavuz Sultan Selim* and *Midilli*, but these ships did not leave Istanbul harbour.

Less distinguished prey then offered itself to the two seaplanes. On August 12th, a merchant ship, hit by British submarines, was hove to and abandoned; Flight Commander Charles Edmonds launched a torpedo from a range of 100 yards and the cargo ship finally sank. Five days later Edmonds inflicted damage on another cargo ship, which had to be towed back to Istanbul, and Flight Commander George B. Dacre completely destroyed an unidentified tug under unusual conditions: forced to touch down because of engine trouble, the pilot released his torpedo while taxiing. The ship went down immediately. It was the first steamship to be destroyed by an aircraft.

However, in spite of these results, the Short 184 was not to be used again for this type of mission. In fact its capabilities were

extremely limited. Once loaded with its torpedo it could only take off in a very calm sea and in a light breeze. Its flying time was restricted to three quarters of an hour, and because of its weight it could not attain an altitude of more than 800 feet. In spite of improvements which produced very satisfactory test results in May 1916, the Short 184 never undertook any further torpedo missions.

The Germans for their part, having tried to develop conventional torpedo-carrying aircraft, also came round to choosing seaplanes. Gotha, starting with the twin-boom WD3, then developed the WD7 with a conventional fuselage. The prototype of this machine, powered by two 120hp Mercedes engines, was delivered in February 1915 for trials which lasted nearly a year, and it was supplied to the German Navy in January 1916. Seven machines of the same type joined it, to be used in training aircrews based on the North Sea. From March 1917 they were followed by the much larger WD11s, which had two 160hp engines. The WD11s operated initially from Flensburg, but some were later sent to bases in the Baltic. The definitive model was the WD14, fitted with two Benz Bz IV 200hp engines, which weighed 10,652lb (nearly 5 tons) with a torpedo and had a maximum speed of 80mph. It went into service in January 1917. The first 16 examples were used for long-range reconnaissance. The Torpedo-Staffel 2 at Zeebrugge became operational on March 25th 1917.

On May 1st 1917 two Gothas sank the *Gena*, a cargo ship of 2,480 tons. One of the Gothas was shot down by light arms fire from the boat, and its crew were taken prisoner. On June 14th the *Kankakee*, 3,720 tons, also went down after some chancy torpedoing from a range of more than a mile and a half. On September 19th the *Storm*, 440 tons, was torpedoed and disappeared beneath the surface in barely two minutes.

These operations stopped at the end of 1917, because

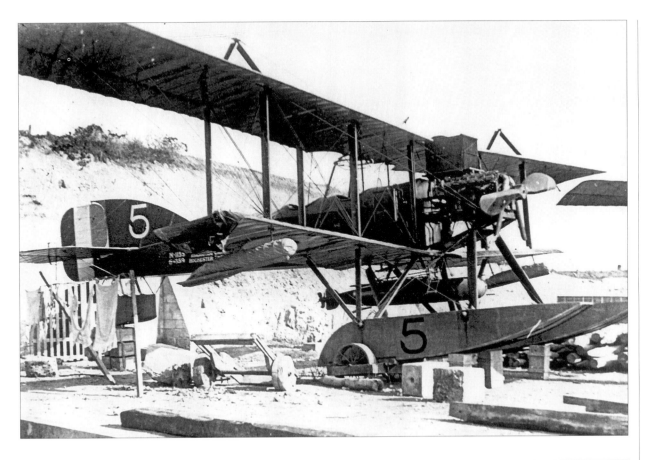

although the Gotha torpedo-carrying seaplanes could take off easily and fly well in calm conditions, taking off in a rough sea was a perilous operation because of the flimsy apparatus fitted for carrying the very heavy load of Whitehead torpedoes. The crew was made up of a pilot, an observer, bomb-aimer and torpedo man, and at the rear a gunner, who was usually left behind in order to save weight. While the aiming and launching equipment proved entirely satisfactory, the gyroscopes on the torpedoes were too easily upset on hitting the water.

Attacks were generally made in bad weather to take advantage of low cloud, and with no warships present (they did not frequent the parts of the English coast attacked) two machines could surprise the merchant ships. Since they flew between 20 and 30 feet above the sea they were soon picked up and subjected to gunfire from the ships, to which they replied with their light armament. The torpedoes were released at least 660 yards from their target.

For the Germans, the results did not justify their losses in men and material, but in retrospect, the British realized that German torpedo-carrying seaplanes could have inflicted heavy losses on British ships if they had been used correctly.

The Short 320 A4 has just launched a Mk IX anti-ship torpedo.

55

THE BATTLE AGAINST THE SUBMARINE

Anti-submarine warfare began in February 1915. The relatively weak German submarine force did not represent a very great threat, but the torpedoing of the *Lusitania* with the death of 1,500 passengers showed that it could not be underestimated. During the summer of 1916 operations were concentrated on the Mediterranean and in the vicinity of the Flemish coast. The Germans rapidly increased their submarine fleet, and on February 1st 1917 it became an all-out war. Combined allied shipping losses, put at 131,000 tons for April 1916, had gone up to 849,000 tons a year later.

The British developed three types of mission for their large Curtiss and Felixstowe flying boats:

– immediate assistance, which meant responding as quickly as possible to a request;

– convoy duty, escorting either convoys or single ships, the missions being carried out at an altitude of 600 feet;

– sea patrols, a routine operation over predetermined sectors, carried out by flying boats at an average altitude of 1,000 feet.

Between April 1917 and November 1918, 312 ships were torpedoed when in convoy, only two of which had air cover. Although effective in ensuring the safety of the convoys, the flying boats turned out to be very disappointing in missions against German submarines: of the 199 sunk, only 7 kills can be

attributed to them.* These very poor results were due to a lack of co-ordination between the ships and the aircraft, and the agitated state of the crews at the moment of attack.

From January 1915 62 H.4 Small Americas were delivered. These were large flying boats, with a wingspan of 70 feet, a length of 33 feet and an all-up weight of 2.2 tons.

The Small America was chronically underpowered, with only 180 or 220hp depending on whether it had Curtiss OX-5 or Clerget engines, and this caused such unflattering comments as: "Here's a comic machine, weighing more than 2 tons, with comic engines giving 180hp (when they actually work) and comic controls. And the poor fellows who attempted incredible feats in them generally had to be taken in tow by the destroyers they were annoying".

These flying boats were mainly used by the Felixstowe school of marine aviation and to carry out tests with a view to the development of the Curtiss H.12 Large America, which was later to see some successes. Larger and more powerful than its predecessor, the H.12 suffered from a weakness in the lower part of the hull, which could give way on takeoff if the sea was at all rough.

Twenty of these machines were delivered to the U.S. Navy, and 71 to the R.N.A.S. On April 24th 1917, just after it had been put into service, an H.12 took part with some ships in an attack on the submarine UB 39. On May 20th 1917, the sinking of UC 36 was the work of a Large America. Four further submarines were sunk between June and September by H.12s; one H.12 was sent to the Mediterranean where German submarines were inflicting heavy losses on the Allies.

A multipurpose machine, the H.12 sometimes took on a pursuit role, even shooting down two Zeppelins, L.22 and L.23. This success is surprising for a flying boat with a wingspan of 92ft 8in and weighing 4½ tons, although it did have four effective machine guns.

The H.16, which followed it, was given a reinforced hull designed by Porte and 375hp Rolls-Royce Eagle engines. Of the 334 made from March 1918 onwards, 30 were in service with the R.A.F. at the end of the war and about 50 with the U.S. Navy. Given convoy escort duties, the H.16 did not record any particular successes.

In fact the most successful machine was the work of Porte himself. He started by converting an H.4, which he fitted with a hull of his own design. The benefits were seen in the Felixstowe F.2A which succeeded it, and which had the wings and tail

The Felixstowe F.2A, designed by John Porte and of which about 100 were built, turned out to be better than its successor.

A real flying fortress, it was successful against other seaplanes and Zeppelins. The strange markings identify N4545 as one of those stationed at Felixstowe.

* The figures quoted come from a comparison of British and German archives. The remarks apply to all the combatants.

section of the H.12. With its new hull the machine made its first flight at the beginning of 1917. It proved to be excellent, the main advantages being a cockpit with dual controls and a flying time of more than nine hours, which enabled it to carry out very long patrols.

From April 1917, all patrol aircraft operated within the 'Spider Web', an octagonal area 60 nautical miles across centred on a marker buoy. By flying to and fro across this area along predetermined lines, a flying boat covered a quarter of the web in three hours, and had a good chance of surprising German submarines on the surface. The big flying boats could drop two 200lb bombs, and the F.2A had impressive defensive armament comprising seven machine guns, which were absolutely essential against the heavy German fighters.

John C. Porte himself piloted the F.2C, a slightly modified version of the basic model, which sank UC 1 on July 24th 1917.

The Felixstowe F.3, which flew in October 1917, carried four 200lb bombs. Its weight made it too slow to engage with the German fighter seaplanes, so it was sent to the Mediterranean. 62 F.3s were delivered before the Armistice.

In France the problem of the anti-submarine battle was tackled differently. The missions allotted to seaplanes remained convoy escort duty carried out by a group of two or three seaplanes, reconnaissance, and also spotting mines in harbour entrance channels.

A remarkable industrial effort enabled the strength of the French naval aviation forces to be increased from 160 units in 1916 to approximately 700 the following year. The seaplanes

were located at centres with between eight and 42 machines and at combat stations with four to six. They were widely distributed – in France, notably in Corsica, in Portugal, in North Africa, in the eastern Mediterranean, and even in Senegal.

The French seaplanes which operated in groups had an active range of 70 miles. As a first stage, they kept the submarines away from the ports; then, in providing cover for the convoys,

Although it could carry twice as many explosives as the F.2 and had a superior range, the Felixstowe F.3 no longer had its predecessor's excellent handling qualities.
It was used solely on anti-submarine patrol missions.

The 92ft 6in wingspan of the Curtiss H.16 Large America is well shown here, as are the protective covers for the engines and propellers, which were very sensitive to salt air.

Even on the water, testing the 47mm cannon on the Tellier produced spectacular effects.

they prevented considerable losses either by deterring the enemy or by disengaging ships from enemy fire. Although they were often described as victories by French propaganda, bombing

attacks on German submarines by the seaplanes of the naval air force did not result in any clear victories. In fact the tiny bombs, sometimes thrown by hand, could not possibly have had any decisive effect.

The French anti-submarine air fleet was made up of the following aircraft: Donnet-Denhaut DD.8 (Hispano-Suiza 200hp) and DD.9 (Hispano-Suiza 300hp); F.B.A. Type H (H-S 150hp) and Type S (H-S 200hp); Lévy-Le Pen HB2 (Renault 300hp); Tellier (H-S 200hp); Tellier-Canon and Tellier with two engines mounted in tandem.

The Lévy-Le Pen was the only one to carry 150lb bombs. The Tellier-Canon had a 37mm cannon which, when fired in flight, practically brought the flying boat to a stop, so powerful was the recoil. Even so it was a weapon which proved well suited to the battle against submarines.

The Germans did not develop any purpose-built machines either. The Hansa-Brandenburg W.12, W.19 and then W.29 effectively demonstrated their versatility by damaging the British submarine C 25 with their machine guns and 20lb bombs, on July 6th 1918.

This Tellier-Canon with two 250hp Hispano-Suiza engines was ironically given the name 'MAD' by its crew, since the cannon had such a devastating effect, not only on the enemy, but also on the airframe of the flying boat because of the recoil.

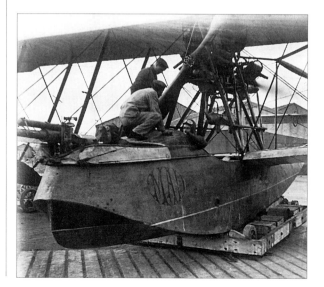

Five Hansa-Brandenburg W.29s from the flight commanded by Friedrich Christiansen attack the British submarine C 25 on July 6th 1918.
This remarkable photograph was taken from the cockpit of one of the attacking aircraft.

SEAPLANES AGAINST SEAPLANES

The First World War was one of the few conflicts in which combat took place between seaplanes, in various theatres of action: in the North Sea, where the Germans based at Zeebrugge and Ostend chalked up a number of successes, and in the Adriatic where the Austrian Gottfried Banfield became an ace with nine confirmed victories.

Combat over the North Sea

German seaplanes were used initially on offensive missions against English ports and shipping. Engaged by Allied aircraft, they recorded their first victory on May 5th 1916 when a Friedrichshafen FF 33H shot down a two-seater Nieuport. The French F.B.A.s based at Dunkirk became easy prey (six were shot down in one month), as were the British Shorts. It was at this time that the distinguished German flyer Friedrich Christiansen began his career; he was to end the war with 20 victories. His very mixed bag included a British airship, seaplanes of all shapes and sizes, a submarine and several high-speed torpedo boats. He was not the only ace from See 1 at Zeebrugge: Ludwig Meyer had six victories to his credit when he disappeared in August 1917.

The first encounter between German seaplanes and an anti-submarine Curtiss took place in May 1917, without any conclusive result one way or the other. About the same time two H.12s shot down the Zeppelins L.22 and L.43. The advent of the Brandenburg W.12s, more powerful and better armed than the FF.33s, enabled Christiansen to shoot down a Porte Baby in October 1917. In December he shot down in flames a British reconnaissance airship, the C. 27, but the first H.12 was shot down by another pilot in February 1918. On April 25th a Felixstowe F.2A and an H.12 were engaged by five W.12s. Christiansen's tactics consisted of putting the rear gunner out of action, then flying alongside the enemy aircraft so that his gunner could fire at the tanks of the port engine. Once the wing was on fire, coming down on the water became a very dangerous business. This is how the Curtiss H.12 no. 8677 disappeared.

On June 4th 1918, four F.2As and an H.12 attacked a formation of 14 German seaplanes. The battle that followed went this way and that, and ended with the loss of two fighters and the capture by the Dutch of two British patrol aircraft. A month later, the arrival of the Brandenburg W.29 led to three F.2As which had attacked five fighters ending up in the sea.

The Hansa-Brandenburg W.12 designed by Ernst Heinkel recorded a victory on December 17th 1917, when Christiansen disposed of the British airship C 27.
The W.12s were the first Hansa-Brandenburg fighters operating from Zeebrugge and could reach 100mph. 146 of them were built.

From 1917 onwards, the heavy German fighter seaplanes proved their aerial supremacy, except when confronted by land-based Sopwith Camels, which were not encumbered with heavy floats.

The Eagle of the Adriatic

Gottfried Banfield had been one of the first aviators in the Austro-Hungarian Kriegsmarine. In two years of fighting he achieved 18 victories, of which only half were credited to him. The first seven were recorded on board a Lohner, an improved version of the F.B.A. bought by the Austrians. His first victim was an Italian balloon, the second a French F.B.A. Type C. The battle took place in the Gulf of Trieste. The first burst of fire killed the Italian observer; the pilot, Vaugeois, then put his machine into a dive, alighted on the water and made for Grado. Banfield pursued him and hit the engine. Vaugeois shot back with his companion's machine gun, but then ran out of ammunition and surrendered. That evening Banfield invited the Frenchman to his table and drank a toast to his bravery. The next day the Austrian aviator was right on the tail of a Macchi L.1, an exact copy of the Lohner, which hit the water hard, and the two members of the crew were injured. Banfield chalked up four victories in August 1916, two

against Italian Caproni Ca.1 bombers and two over French Type H F.B.A.s. His last victories were achieved in a Brandenburg CC against a Ca.1, and in an Oeffag Type H over an Italian seaplane, unidentified because the engagement took place at night. Banfield was thus the first Austrian fighter pilot to record a victory at night. Having become the most highly decorated Austrian pilot, he received the title of Freiherr (baron) on August 16th 1917, a unique distinction for an aviator in the First World War.

At the end of the war, the three-seater W.29 displayed formidable versatility and efficiency.

The Brandenburg CC no.946 was designed by Camilo Castiglioni for Gottfried Banfield, who claimed three victories with this machine between October and December 1916, one of which was against a Caproni Ca.1.
The machine could reach 110mph. Twenty six were delivered to the Kriegsmarine.

CHAPTER 3

The Golden Age

BETWEEN 1919 AND 1938, MARINE AVIATION DEVELOPED IN INDUSTRIALIZED COUNTRIES, BECAUSE IN MANY PARTS OF THE WORLD SEAPLANES OFFERED POSSIBILITIES NOT AVAILABLE TO THEIR LAND-BASED EQUIVALENTS. THE DEVELOPMENT OF RACING SEAPLANES CULMINATED IN 1934 IN AN ABSOLUTE SPEED RECORD OF 440MPH.

A Loening C-2-C moored in the Bay of Avalon (left).

The seaplanes designed for racing, with their reduced dimensions and extremely powerful engines, were marvels of engineering

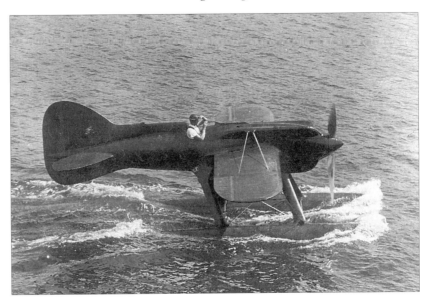

After the war the trophy for seaplanes put up by Jacques Schneider was to have an extraordinary impact during the twelve years of the competition, not only on the development of marine aviation but also on that of the engines and aerodynamics.

The third competition took place at Bournemouth on September 10th 1919. In spite of thick fog, the organizers allowed the four competitors to start. The three Britons crashed or gave up in the course of the 10 laps required. Guido Jannello completed 11 laps, but he had used a reserve marker as his guide. He was first disqualified, then declared the winner. Eventually the competition was annulled but Italy was given the task of organizing the next event. The French were notable by their absence, since the Nieuport 29 G and the Spad-Herbemont S.20 were not ready to tackle the rigours of the competition.

The next year's event in Venice on September 20th 1920 was again a fiasco. The Italians had decided that the machines should carry a weight of 660lb. The only starter was a Savoia S.12bis, which covered the 230 miles at an average speed of 105.5mph. The Spad-Herbemont, Macchi M.12 and Savoia S.19 did not even put in an appearance.

On August 11th 1921, again in Venice, two Macchi M.7s and an M.19 fought it out; the event was finally won by the M.7 of Giovanni de Briganti at an average of 118mph. He was also the only finisher. Several entrants had to give up before the start, including a Nieuport 29.

On August 12th 1922 in the event at Naples, the Supermarine Sea Lion II of Henri Biard came home the winner in front of three Italians at an average of 145.7mph. It was only a narrow victory over Alessandro Passaleva, who was piloting a Savoia S.51. For the first time the four competitors all finished at a speed of 200kph (124mph) or over.

The Curtiss Racer R2C-2 was prepared for the 1924 Schneider Trophy, but the race did not take place. It could fly at a speed of 227mph.

Lieutenant David Rittenhouse at
the controls of his Curtiss
CR-3 A 6081, who was to win in
1923 at an average of
176.9mph.

Lieutenant David Rittenhouse at
the controls of his Curtiss
CR-3 A 6081, who was to win in
1923 at an average of
176.9mph.

The Supermarine Sea Lion I
piloted by Basil Hobbs (below
left) sank in its first event, after
holing the hull in the fog.

The CAMS 38 piloted by
Maurice Hurel in the 1923
competition retired on the
second lap, eliminating France
from the Schneider Trophy.

On September 28th 1923 the race took place at Cowes on the Isle of Wight, in brilliant sunshine and with a calm sea. Three countries were represented: Britain with a Supermarine Sea Lion III, France with a CAMS 38 which gave up at the start, and the United States with two Curtiss CR-3s, real racing seaplanes which outclassed the rest of the field. Lieutenant David Rittenhouse came first at an average of 177mph, followed by Lieutenant Irvine at 173mph.

Two years later the speed of winner James Doolittle was 30% higher. At the controls of a Curtiss R3C-2 specially designed for the U.S. Navy, this legendary pilot covered the 217 miles of the race at 232.6mph, more than 30mph faster than the second man

James Doolittle with his Curtiss R3C-2, winner of the 1925 Baltimore event at an average of 232mph.
With the same aircraft he took the air speed record over 2 miles to 250.8mph on October 27th 1925.

The Macchi M.33 finished third and last in the 1925 Schneider Trophy, at a speed more than 60mph slower than the winner's.

home, the Briton Hubert Broad. Curtiss had done a wonderful job on the streamlining of his biplane, since his engine only developed 565hp as compared with the 700hp of the Gloster IIIA. A third machine completed the event at Baltimore on October 26th 1925, a Macchi M.33 which was completely outclassed. This was to be the last flying boat to take part in a Schneider Trophy race.

On November 13th 1926 the contest at Hampton Roads was reduced to an Italian-American affair: three Macchi M.39s were opposed by three Curtisses. A splendid scrap between Mario de Bernardi and George Cuddihy in an R3C-4 ended in favour of the Italian, who took every risk on the last lap while the Curtiss ran out of fuel.

The winner had completed the course at an average of 246.5mph as compared with 231mph for Frank Schilt in an R3C-2 and 218mph for Adriano Bacula in a Macchi M.39. Designed by Mario Castoldi, the Macchi M.39 was a braced monoplane fitted with a Fiat AS.2 engine giving 800hp. With this machine de Bernardi broke the air speed record on November 17th 1926 at 258.87mph, with a recorded speed at one point of 272.6mph.

A year later, on September 26th 1927, the massed spectators on the Venice Lido witnessed an Anglo-Italian contest. Three Macchi M.52s, derived from the M.39 and capable of accepting a Fiat AS.3 engine giving 1,000hp, faced a Gloster IVB and two Supermarine S.5s. Only the S.5s completed the course. S.N. Webster won at an average of 281.65mph from O.E. Worsley

The extraordinarily clean lines of the Italian monoplanes entered from 1926 onwards were the work of the engineer Castoldi.
The Macchi M.39 won at Baltimore at an average of 246mph.

The three Macchi M.52s entered at Venice in 1927 did not finish the race due to faults with their 1,000hp engines.

67

To get the racing seaplanes off the water without flaps meant very long runs in a straight line.

The Supermarine S.5 won in 1927 and was third in 1929 at Calshot.

(273mph) although his Napier Lion engine had slightly less power (875hp as against 900hp).

Reginald Mitchell had been responsible for the S.5's design, with centrally placed, braced wings, radiators moulded into the wings, and uprated engines. The superiority of the Supermarine was such that the British entered an S.5 and two S.6s on September 7th 1929 at Calshot to compete against an M.52R and two M.67s. The main change was in the engines, the power of which was doubled for the new aircraft. H.R.D. Waghorn came first in an S.6 fitted with a Rolls-Royce R engine producing 1,800hp, at an average of 328.63mph; the second S.6 was disqualified for not going round a pylon, but its speed was only slightly lower.

The secret of the British success lay in the high-powered Rolls-Royce engines

A Supermarine S.6A fitted with a 1,900hp engine is flanked by two S.6Bs powered by the 2,300hp Rolls-Royce R unit, R.

The Macchi M.67s did not finish, while the M.52R and the S.5 of the earlier generation were more than 40mph slower than the leading aircraft.

In 1924 the Americans had cancelled the event because they had no one to compete against. They would have been certain to win the competition, and hence the Schneider Trophy, in perpetuity since the competition's regulations stipulated three consecutive wins.

The British did not show the same sporting spirit. At Calshot on September 13th 1931, John Boothman was the only starter in a Supermarine S.6B, and covered the 217 miles at an average speed of 340mph, so Great Britain took possession of the the Schneider Trophy. To add some meaning to this hollow victory, the second S.6B set up a new absolute air speed record on the same day of 379mph.

Originally devised to promote air travel over the oceans, the Schneider Trophy became transformed into a pure speed competition. Due to its international character, it brought about engine improvements to the tune of a five-fold increase in power over 12 years, and also revolutionized aerodynamics and the construction of airframes. Not being limited to a certain distance for takeoff and landing, the racing seaplanes dispensed with flaps, which made it possible to have very thin wing profiles.

Launching the Supermarine S.6B S1595, which, as the only competitor in the 1931 race, gave Britain the Schneider Trophy in perpetuity with three consecutive victories.
James Boothman recorded an average of 340mph.

As a direct consequence of the competition, the Macchi MC.72, with a 3,000hp engine that was at last reliable, took the air speed record from the Supermarine S.6B on October 23rd 1934 at 440.68mph, streets ahead of any other landplane of the day. This record still stands today for seaplanes with piston engines. And as an indirect consequence, but more importantly, Reginald Mitchell's research work on the S.4 to S.6B seaplanes was to provide the starting point for the design of the famous Spitfire fighter.

The most extraordinary performance achieved by a racing seaplane took place on October 23rd 1934, when di Agello attained the speed of 440mph in a Macchi MC.72 powered by a 3,000hp engine.
This record still stands in the piston-engined seaplane category.

The Curtiss NC-4 receives all the mechanics' attention as they check over the engines before the Atlantic crossing.

THE FIRST CROSSING OF THE NORTH ATLANTIC

The fascination exerted by the Atlantic crossing was revived in 1919. The U.S. Navy had brought out a seaplane in 1918 capable of accompanying convoys as far as the mid-Atlantic. This was NC-1, built by Curtiss. In November 1918 the machine had carried 51 passengers and crew, which was a record. Four were made, with the aim of winning the *Daily Mail* prize. NC-2 donated parts to repair NC-1 and did not take part in the flight. Leaving Rockaway Beach, New York, on May 8th 1919, NC-1 and NC-3 arrived at Trepassey Bay, Newfoundland, two days later, while NC-4 had to taxi on the water for 60 miles to reach Cape Cod, where an engine was changed. It rejoined the other two Curtisses on May 15th. The next day the three flying boats set course for the Azores. NC-1 came down in the open sea with wave troughs 20 feet deep; the crew were not equal to the struggle and were rescued by a cargo ship. NC-3 touched down in the sea 200 miles from Horta, which it reached after battling with the elements for two days. NC-4 arrived at Horta after a flight of 19hrs 30mins, just before a thick fog descended on the area. Delayed by having to wait for the other two flying boats, Lieutenant Commander Read reached Lisbon on May 27th, thus completing the first crossing of the Atlantic by air. NC-4 continued its flight to Plymouth, touching down on May 31st.

In a total flying time of 57 hours, NC-4 had made it from New York to Plymouth, a feat which pointed towards a future for marine aviation as a means of transport.

Of the four machines that set off, NC-4 was the only one to reach Lisbon, on May 27th 1919.
Lieutenant-Commander Read's crew look very tired. The four-engined aircraft needed almost 60 flying hours from New York to Plymouth, which it reached on May 31st. The feat of NC-4 in making the first aerial crossing of the Atlantic opened up new perspectives for the use of flying boats.

A HYBRID FOR
THE FIRST AERIAL CIRCUMNAVIGATION OF THE GLOBE

In the hope of promoting military aviation by means of a spectacular event, in 1923 General Mitchell suggested trying a trip round the world with an aircraft which could be fitted with floats. Four of the Douglas World Cruisers (DWCs) were built, and they left Santa Monica on March 17th 1924. The floats were fitted at Seattle.

One machine was lost in Alaska, but the other three continued on their journey, which took them to Tokyo, Shanghai, Saigon and Calcutta, where the floats came off again. They crossed the Indies and the Middle East and arrived in Paris on July 14th, then reached London, and refitted the floats at Brough for the Atlantic crossing. A second DWC broke up during a rescue operation attempted by a cruiser. The weather conditions over Iceland were appalling, so that the two survivors did not reach Newfoundland until September 2nd. The wheels were finally replaced, and after a triumphant crossing of the United States the two DWCs arrived at Seattle via San Francisco on September 28th 1924. In 175 days, they had covered 28,926 miles, and flown for 371 hours at an average of 77.6mph.

It is interesting to compare the performance of the DWC with and without floats (the figures in brackets are for the version without floats):
- maximum speed 100mph (103mph);
- landing speed 53mph (37mph);
- ceiling 6,600 feet (10,000 feet);
- range 1,650 miles (2,300 miles);

The floats added 660lb to the dry weight, or a fifth of the total weight. It can be concluded from this that with the exception of the distance that could be covered non-stop, which in the event did not exceed 870 miles, the differences seem to be quite negligible for this class of aircraft.

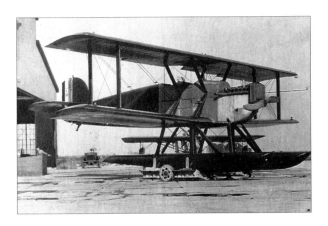

The Douglas World Cruiser could only make its round the world trip with the aid of removable floats, a device frequently used from the beginnings of marine aviation.
The additional drag and weight hardly affected the performance of this machine, which was to bring Donald Douglas a worldwide reputation.

The crew of this Portuguese Navy Dornier Wal try out the emergency mast and sail in preparation for an endurance flight from Lisbon to Buenos Aires in 1927.

The Dornier Wal used by Amundsen and then by von Gronau for his first crossing of the North Atlantic is returned to the Deutsches Museum.

It has touched down on a snowy Munich Airport, a reminder of its landing on the polar ice in 1925.

THE DORNIER WAL

Both the Curtiss NC-4 and the DWC were conceived as experimental machines. The Dornier Do-J Wal on the other hand, although it undertook many spectacular flights, was produced in large numbers for both military and civil purposes.

Derived from the Gs 1 made during the war, the Wal's characteristic feature was the lateral fin placed under the wings to stabilize the rolling of the hull, which obviated the need for floats. It first flew on November 6th 1922 in Italy, where Dornier were able to escape the constraints of the Treaty of Versailles.

The Spaniard Ramon Franco was responsible for the Wal's first feat, flying from Spain to the Canaries in January 1924. The explorer Roald Amundsen tried to fly over the North Pole in May 1925. His two Wals reached latitude 87° 43', but one had to be abandoned. All the expedition returned to Spitzbergen in the surviving Wal after spending weeks trapped in the ice.

On January 22nd 1926 Ramon Franco took off from Palos de Moguer in the Plus Ultra, and in seven stages reached Buenos Aires on February 10th. The first crossing of the South Atlantic from east to west had taken 60 hours flying time to cover 6,378 miles. Epic journeys followed one after another, the most remarkable being the flight by a group of three Dutch Wal machines delivered to Indonesia, a marathon of 9,688 miles completed between April 3rd and May 18th 1929. Wolfgang von Gronau was responsible for the Wal's last exploits 10 years after its first flight, numerous improvements having been made in the interim. Between August 18th and 22nd 1930 he flew from the Baltic to New York via Iceland, Greenland, Labrador and Montreal, the 4,223 miles being covered in 44 hours flying time. He did it again the following year, then between July and November 1932 he completed a trip round the world of 27,572 miles in 270 hours of flying.

With all these epic performances the Dornier Wal confirmed its qualities, and proved that the idea of regular services by flying boats on transoceanic routes merited serious consideration.

The Japanese bought Dornier Wal no. 59 straight off the production line. Fitted with two 360hp Rolls-Royce Eagle IX engines, it carried eight passengers between the islands and covered the Fukuoka-Shanghai route.

The Dornier Wal, when fitted with 600hp BMW engines, could fly at 121mph, an improvement of 12mph over the the Eagle engines. The Wal was fitted with 15 different types of engine in the course of its career.

THE EXPLOITS OF ITALO BALBO

The Savoia-Marchetti S.55, which first flew in August 1924, was one of the great successes of marine aviation and one of the most original designs of its day. Intended as a bomber and torpedo aircraft, this twin-hull, twin-engined machine had a production run of 200, of which about 20 were used on commercial routes. An ideal propaganda vehicle, the S.55 made some outstanding flights over a period of seven years, showing a longevity worthy of the Dornier Wal.

On February 13th 1927, the Marquis de Pinedo took off from Sardinia and arrived on the 27th at Rio de Janeiro. He turned north to the United States, where his flying boat was accidentally set on fire. He left New York on May 8th in a second machine for Rome, where he received a hero's welcome on June 16th.

The Italians then tried flights in large formations: in 1928 61 flying boats managed to cover 3,000km (1,863 miles) over the Mediterranean, then in 1929, 35 S.55As made a flight of 5,000km (3,105 miles) to the Black Sea. They foreshadowed the more ambitious flights of General Italo Balbo, who became Air Minister at the age of 34. Twelve S.55As left Orbetello on December 17th 1930. By Christmas, they had reached Portuguese Guinea. On January 6th 1931, 14 machines (the two tender aircraft having joined up) launched an assault on the South Atlantic. Two machines were lost at the outset, two were missing on arrival, so ten flew over the Brazilian town of Natal in formation.

Italo Balbo's greatest exploit was his Rome-Chicago flight with a squadron of 24 S.55Xs, a version with a more powerful engine. They took off on July 1st 1933. The long trip started with a crossing of the Alps to reach Amsterdam, where one of the aircraft turned over. It was replaced by the tender aircraft. Then after several stages, of which the longest was 1,428 miles, all the S.55Xs reached Chicago in formation on July 15th. After a short stay in America, the return flight took the southerly route via the Azores. As a result of an accident on takeoff from Horta, it was in

The S.I.A.I. S.55X was specially adapted to fly the North Atlantic.
Its Isotta-Fraschini Asso engines mounted in tandem, each giving 750hp, enabled it to fly from Orbetello to Chicago in stages, taking 48hrs 47mins flying time and averaging 124.2mph.

The crews of the S.55As, although in the shelter of their cockpits, were still very close to the engines.

The instrument panel of an S.55A of the Balbo squadron seems particularly austere.
The dual control for the pilots offered a certain degree of safety, and the crew could get to the floats..

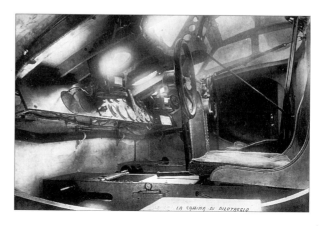

Line-up of the Balbo squadron at Orbetello before leaving for the South Atlantic.

the end 23 machines which touched down at Ostia on August 12th. Balbo received a triumphant welcome and was promoted to the rank of Air Marshal, an honour that was richly deserved for the leadership qualities he had shown when the seaplanes were caught in the fog between Iceland and Labrador. Balbo's flights demonstrated that, given meticulous organization, seaplanes were technically and practically capable of making flights across the oceans.

With its strange configuration, the S.55A did not achieve its reputation by virtue of its looks, but at the beginning of its career it was far ahead of any rival machines.
Air Marshal Balbo demonstrated its reliability in a whole series of carefully prepared endurance flights.

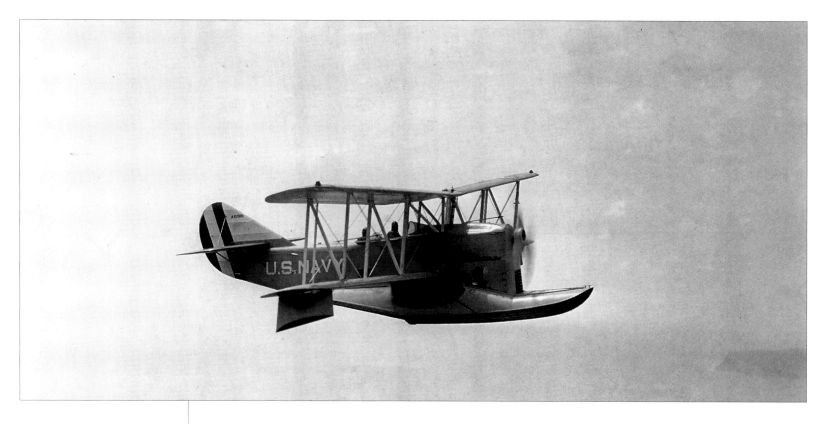

A Loening OL-2 of the MacMillan Arctic Expedition during a test flight over the bay at San Diego, California.

Loening OL-4s operated from the beaches of Ketchikan in Alaska, in particularly difficult conditions for the crews and mechanics.
Fortunately the Loening was very robust.

A VERY WILLING AMPHIBIAN

Among all the multipurpose flying boats built in the twenties, the Loening Amphibian has a special place as one of the first amphibians to go into series production. The characteristic feature of this biplane with its aggressive lines was the large central float on which the fuselage rested, and which had the landing gear built into it. The first example made its maiden flight on June 9th 1924 from the East River, New York.

Ordered by the U.S.A.F., U.S. Navy, the Marine Corps, the U.S. Coast Guard, airline companies and private owners, the Amphibian was to take part in numerous long-distance and exploration flights.

Between June 20th and October 11th 1925, three OL-2s made photographic reconnaissance flights along the coasts of Labrador and Greenland for the U.S. Navy. On December 21st the U.S.A.F. made a demonstration flight with five OA-1As. The Loenings started from Texas and flew via Mexico down to Santiago in Chile, following the Pacific coast. On February 24th 1927 they became the first seaplanes to fly over the Andes in formation, covering the 650 miles between Valdivia and Bahìa Blanca in six hours. Returning via the West Indies, the Loenings reached Washington where they touched down on May 2nd, after covering 21,592 miles in 263 hours, at an average speed of 82mph. The OA-1As had touched down 65 times on the water before returning to dry land, under their own power for most of the time.

As a result of this flight, the Loening's future was assured. It became the first machine bought by the American coastguards and it was even to be found in Hanoi as well as in China, where a version carrying six passengers flew between Peking and Chungking at a time of great unrest.

The configuration developed by Loening was also to be used on the amphibian built by Grumman, a company of which Grover Loening was a co-founder.

THE LINDBERGHS GO BY SEAPLANE

Although his New York-Paris flight had already brought Charles Lindbergh to the pinnacle of fame at the age of 25, his aerial adventures did not stop there. Paradoxically his role as adviser, initially to Transcontinental Air Transport (which soon became TWA) and then at the same time to Pan American, was to have much more important consequences for the history of aviation. Thanks to his clear vision, his technical advice was perfectly presented and allowed his employers to make rapid progress over a period of more than 20 years. It was for Pan American

that Lindbergh became an enthusiastic seaplane pilot.

On February 4th 1929, he made the first mail flight between Miami and the Panama Canal, a distance of 2,300 miles, in five stages. On this occasion he used the second Sikorsky S-38, a twin-boom amphibian carrying nine passengers or one ton of freight. The machine, nicknamed 'Ugly Duckling', arrived at its destination two days later. On its return, Lindbergh's forthcoming marriage was announced to Anne Morrow, the daughter of the United States ambassador to Mexico,. Combining business with pleasure, the couple made an exploratory flight to the West

Charles Lindbergh poses for the cameras, with Basil Rowe (in the leather helmet) and the mailbags which they are about to carry from Panama to Miami with the Sikorsky S.38 amphibian.

Crouched on one of the floats, Lindbergh carefully supervises the fitting of trolleys which will allow his Lockheed Sirius to be brought out of the water at Copenhagen.

Indies with a view to establishing a mail service between the islands. In Trinidad the Lindberghs left their companions to go off on their own – for their honeymoon.

Still in an S-38, Lindbergh inaugurated the mail flight from Miami to Buenos Aires and back, between April 26th and May 2nd 1930. Then, leaving the Americas for a while, he used a Lockheed 8 Sirius to make a series of survey flights accompanied by his wife.

Designed by Jerry Vultee, the Sirius started its career as a landplane, with which the Lindberghs set up a transcontinental speed record between California and New York, but for these flights it was fitted with two metal floats made by Edo and containing fuel tanks.

From July 27th to October 2nd 1931 the two aviators explored the possible routes in the North Pacific via Alaska, Japan and China. An unfortunate accident when hoisting the machine halted the journey on the Yangtse Kiang. Back home in California, the machine was given a more powerful engine for a new programme of flights, this time over the Atlantic. The routes via the Azores and via Greenland forming the 'great circle' were explored in turn. The Eskimos gave the aircraft the name 'Tingmissartoq' – 'that which flies like a big bird'. After a series of flights in Europe, including an obligatory call at Paris, the Sirius flew down to Bathurst (now Banjul) in Gambia, from where it made a crossing of the South Atlantic, the flight to Natal taking nearly 16 hours.

SERVING THE TRUE EXPLORERS

Initially used on exploratory flights by Pan American, the S-38 quickly became a success in both military and civil aviation, and more than 100 were built. S-38BS Osa's Ark belonging to the explorers Osa and Martin Johnson achieved great fame, which it was to share with the Spirit of Africa.

With pith helmets planted on their heads and cameras at the ready, the Johnsons introduced Americans to the splendours of Africa as seen from the air, in particular Kilimanjaro.

The two pilots Carstens and Sergievsky made flights that were right on the safety limit. However when Vern Carstens recalled his two years with S-38BS, it was with real pleasure:

"Certainly taking off from the water always caused problems, because the spray whipped up by the slipstream of the propellers was thrown onto the cockpit windows. Visibility was nil until the amphibian rose onto the hull step. After that, taking off was simple. Even with a strong cross wind, touching down on the water turned out to be easy, as the hull had been particularly well designed.

Moving either on the water or on land wasn't a problem. The landing speed of 50mph made it possible to use runways less than 500 yards long. Because of the altitude and the tropical conditions we were careful about weight on takeoff, but if the conditions were favourable we didn't hesitate to exceed the recommended figures, and the way the S-38 took off gave the impression that it could lift any load. As for its flying qualities, they gave no cause for criticism.

In the very basic conditions in Kenya, maintenance didn't present any insurmountable problems, and it was enough to open the hatches to dry out the floats, the wings and the interior of the cabin, as long as it wasn't salt water."

Wearing a splendid pith helmet, Osa Johnson supervises maintenance work on his Sikorsky S.38 on a stopover at Le Bourget in July 1934.
The machine with its strange markings was nicknamed *Osa's Ark.*

Boarding an F.B.A. 19 HMT 3 which the Air Union company used experimentally on its routes to England. The machine took three passengers sitting in an open cockpit.

The CAMS 53-1 F-AJIS belonging to Air Union went into service on the Marseilles-Beirut run in 1929. The machine had a range of 620 miles and the 2,018-mile journey took three days. The CAMS was also used on the Marseilles-Algiers route.

COMMERCIAL OPERATION OF FRENCH SEAPLANES

The development of the commercial use of seaplanes between the wars followed the same pattern in all those countries with an aviation industry, with the exception of Germany which was shackled by the Treaty of Versailles. Commercial air transport, which initially used war surplus machines adapted to a greater or lesser extent, only survived thanks to the subsidies granted by the government for carrying mail. The passengers were unable to pay the real cost: they came as an extra in addition to the freight, and were faced with spartan conditions.

In 1919 about a dozen companies came into being. Among those which only used seaplanes, the Guyanese Transport Company flew 14 Lévy-Le Pens and five Breguet 14T bis Hs until 1921, Franco-Bilbaine used about 20 Lévy-Le Pen and 200hp Hispano-powered Tellier flying boats, and l'Aéronavale put three Donnet D.9s into service, which were used until 1925 between Antibes and Ajaccio. In spite of the subsidies received per kilometre, the first two companies soon went bankrupt. The old single-engined marine reconnaissance aircraft were not up to the demands of a regular service.

In the Mediterranean

The air transport companies at that time restricted French flying boats to the task of opening up new routes, or used them to experiment with regular services for carrying mail in the South Atlantic and passengers in the Mediterranean. This was how the first flying boats conceived specifically by Aéronavale with accommodation for four passengers came into being: the Lioré et Olivier LeO H.13, which went into service on the Antibes-Ajaccio run, before covering the Marseilles-Algiers route for a subsidiary

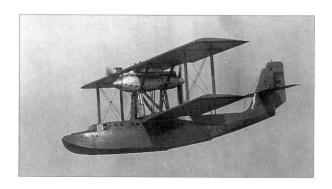

of the Latécoère airlines. It had only a limited performance, and a large number of the 32 built were lost. The twin-engined Latécoère Laté 21 was hardly any more successful; incapable of flying on one engine, three of the five machines operating the Marseilles-Algiers route were lost in a few months. It was gradually replaced by the LeO H.190 and its derivatives. It carried six passengers instead of its predecessor's four, which was not enough to ensure that it would be profitable in operation. After testing the three-engined SPCA Météore, Aéropostale (the air mail service) decided to buy nine Laté 32s, which were delivered from 1927 on, as well as eight CAMS 53s and four CAMS 56s. At the same time, Aéronavale (which became Air Union in 1926) bought a series of ten CAMS 53-1s which it put into service on the Marseilles-Tunisia route from 1929 on. Ten further CAMS 53s went to Air Union's Orient Lines, which opened the Marseilles-Beirut route on June 6th 1929, the longest route in the world operated by flying boats with a distance of 2,018 miles.

The CAMS 53, of which 31 were built in three different versions by the Chantiers aéronautiques de la Seine between 1933 and 1938, was a flying boat made of wood and canvas, with twin engines in tandem, 48ft 7ins long with a wingspan of 67ft. Its 500hp Hispano-Suiza 12Hbr engines gave a cruising speed of 105mph, the maximum speed being up to 137mph. Its maximum range was 620 miles. The well-equipped cabin took four passengers in addition to a crew consisting of a pilot, a co-pilot and a radio operator. Three machines designated CAMS 56 were fitted with different engines and structurally lightened.

In all, 22 machines were flown by the amalgamation of French airlines called Air France from 1933 on. Of the 34 CAMS 53s and 56s, 15 were destroyed as a result of accidents, and six damaged. On the Marseilles-Algiers route the aircraft were pushed to the limit of what they could do. On the other hand, on the Tunisian and eastern routes the possibility of touching down close to islands or coasts made these journeys easier. Here the

The Breguet 530 Saigon used on the Marseilles-Ajaccio-Tunis route from January 1935 had the peculiarity of offering three classes of accommodation: second class at the front for 11 passengers, first class in the middle for six, and three seats in a separate luxury cabin.

**Lioré et Olivier LeO H.242 no.1
flies over the Marseilles docks.**
Fourteen H.242 and H.242-1
machines were used by Air France
on all their Mediterranean routes
to carry up to 15 passengers.

CAMS 53s proved themselves to be entirely satisfactory.

The Lioré et Olivier LeO H.242 took their place in 1934. Originally only two were built, but in the end there were to be 12 of the heavier H.242-1, which was also capable of operating over longer distances. Fitted with four Gnome Rhône Titan Major 350hp engines mounted in tandem, the H.242 had a metal hull made of anodized Duralumin, whereas the wings were still made of a wooden frame covered in plywood. Used on all the Mediterranean routes, the 14 machines carried between 10 and 15 passengers depending on weather conditions, at a maximum speed of 143mph and with a range of 680 miles. Two H.242-1s were still being used by Air France in 1942.

From January 1935, the national airline also used two Breguet 530 Saigons, which were Short Calcuttas that had been modified by the French manufacturer. These three-engined biplanes could carry 11 second class passengers, six first class and three in a luxury-class cabin.

Air France asked Lioré et Olivier to think of a successor for the H.242-1. The H.246, which was on the programme for 1935, flew for the first time in September 1937. This prototype was followed by six H.246-1s built by the SNCASE, which had absorbed Lioré et Olivier, in February 1937. The hull, which benefited from the studies for the H.47, was made in the same

way as that of the H.242, while the plywood-covered wings housed four 720hp Hispano-Suiza 12 Xir engines. The H.246-1 carried 26 passengers with a range of 930 miles. In October 1939 Air France inaugurated the Marseilles-Algiers route with the new flying boat, which carried 27 passengers, more than half a ton of freight and 900lb of mail. The cruising speed of the H.246-1 was 160mph and its maximum 208mph, which, combined with the increased number of passengers, improved the flying boat's profitability. Two examples were to survive the war and resume their Mediterranean service in September 1944. They were finally retired in September 1946, thus ending the story of French flying boats in the Mediterranean.

In the South Atlantic

The real ambition of Marcel Bouilloux-Laffont, who bought out the C.G.E.A. (the Latécoère airlines) in April 1927, was to create an airline giving a continuous service between Paris and Santiago in Chile. The air crossing of the South Atlantic by the Dakar-Natal route was the main obstacle, with 1,972 miles of ocean to cross in one go. The company decided to use a Laté 28-3 seaplane for the first attempt.

This machine with two floats belonged to the Laté 28 series, a land-based aircraft used with success and in numbers on the

The LeO H.246, here in prototype form, had a much better performance than its predecessor. Three of them were taken by the Germans.

It was with the Latécoère 28-3 *Comte de la Vaulx* that Mermoz made the first crossing of the South Atlantic with mail on May 12th 1930.

He was accompanied on the 21-hour flight by navigator Dabry and radio operator Gimié.

The Latécoère 300 *Croix du Sud* touches down at Sartrouville shortly after breaking numerous distance records.

It was in this elegant four-engined aircraft that Mermoz disappeared on December 7th 1936.

coasts of Africa. It was fitted with a single 600hp Hispano-Suiza 12Lb6 engine which enabled it to reach a maximum of 137mph and a cruising speed of 100mph. The choice of a single-engined aircraft seems on the face of it rather foolhardy, but the Laté 28-3 named *Comte de La Vaulx* established 13 world records, including a flight of 2,609 miles over a closed circuit with a load of half a ton, which proved that the machine had a good safety margin.

On May 12th 1930 at 10.56am, Mermoz, Dabry and Gimié took off from Saint Louis in Senegal with the mail that had left Toulouse the day before. This was not an endurance flight, but a commercial test flight. Apart from 3½ hours in the doldrums and problems with the oil pressure, the flight went without incident.

The *Comte de la Vaulx* touched down at 8.20am, having been in the air for 21hrs 24mins. The letters arrived in Buenos Aires in less than four days thanks to this feat, which however owed a lot to good luck.

The return attempt ended in failure. On July 10th the Laté 28-3 sank close to a repair vessel, which picked up the crew safe and sound as well as the mail. Aéropostale gave up its ambitious plans to use a single-engined seaplane. Although it gained him unequalled popularity, Mermoz's exploit was not to be repeated.

It was not until 1934 that Aéropostale began to use multi-engined flying boats, first the Laté 300 Croix du Sud, which flew from Saint Louis to Natal for the first time on January 3rd, and then the Blériot 5190 Santos-Dumont on November 27th.

The Laté 300 *Croix du Sud* was a four-engined aircraft with a large sponson float, and a wingspan of 145 feet. Its total weight fully loaded at 22½ tons was double its unladen weight, its maximum speed was 130mph and it could cover a distance of 3,000 miles nonstop. In the hands of pilots from the French Navy before being passed to Air France, it made six crossings with mail in 1934, 12 the following year and six in 1936. On December 7th 1936 Mermoz with a crew of four took off from Dakar. Four hours later the radio gave out the message: "Let's cut the starboard rear engine." And then nothing. The Laté 300 had disappeared without trace. All France mourned the loss of its hero, Jean Mermoz.

Derived from the Laté 300, the Laté 301 came into service on December 30th 1935. Called *Ville de Buenos Aires*, it made three crossings before disappearing over the sea on February 10th 1936. The *Ville de Santiago* made 18 crossings in 1936, as did the *Ville de Rio de Janeiro*, which added another eight in 1937.

The Blériot 5190 made its first flight on August 11th 1933: it was a large four-engined aircraft with a high wing connected to the hull by the superstructure housing the crew. Its cruising speed was up to 116mph and it had a range of 2,000 miles with more than half a ton of freight and against a headwind of 30mph. It flew from Dakar to Natal for the first time on November 27th 1934, and had made a total of 38 crossings when Air France decided in 1938 not to use flying boats on this route any more.

The Farman 220 and 2200 were in fact proving much more efficient. However, from 1930 to 1937 the Blériots had made 111 transoceanic mail flights, 10 out of the 16 in 1934, 35 out of the 42 in 1935, 48 out of the 86 the following year, but only 16 out of the 104 in 1937. They had had the important and difficult task of honing the techniques and practical procedures before giving way to higher performance machinery, as had also been the case in other countries.

COMMERCIALLY OPERATED GERMAN SEAPLANES

It may seem strange that Germany developed its own seaplane operations when one considers its geographical situation. However, the Baltic fulfilled the same purpose for Germany as the Mediterranean did for France, and the South Atlantic was just as much of an obstacle to investments in Latin America.

The technical quality of German goods having made the country an important exporter, this justified the construction of a prestige flying boat, the Do X, which symbolized the new strength of German marine aviation.

A noble line

Having gained valuable experience during the war in the development of large flying boats, Claudius Dornier set to work on the conversion of the Gs 1 into a transport aircraft. This new model saw the birth of the formula that was to be repeated in a whole line of machines developed by Dornier: a wide metal hull which is intrinsically stable, fitted with lateral fins supporting wings mounted high up to escape the spray. The Gs 1 made its first flight on July 31st 1919, under test by Ad Astra Aero, a Swiss air transport company. The Allied Commission considered that it could too easily be converted into a bomber, and it was destroyed on their insistence on April 25th 1920.

In order not to run this risk again, Dornier set up a factory on the Swiss shore of Lake Constance. It was from here on November 24th 1920 that the Cs II took off. Designed to carry five passengers, the all-metal Delphin (Dolphin) I was bought by the U.S. Navy, who studied its all-metal construction, and then by Japan. The next two examples, the much improved Delphin II and Delphin III, were made in Italy and used experimentally for pleasure flights.

Claudius Dornier's great success was the Do J Wal (Whale), which first flew on November 6th 1922. Three hundred were

made if one includes all versions, both civilian and military, up to 1936. It was easily the greatest commercial success in the history of marine aviation. The first order for 20 machines came from the Spanish navy, then the Do J was built in Italy for the S.C.A.D.T.A., a German-Colombian company which operated three from 1925 on; 16 went to the S.A.N.A. (S.A. di Navigazione Aerea) and 10 to the S.A. Aero Espresso Italiana, which used them in the Mediterranean; four went to Deutscher Aero Lloyd to fly over the Baltic before being handed over to Deutsche Lufthansa (D.L.H.), who in the course of several years bought

After the First World War Claudius Dornier built this metal monster, the Do L Dolphin I, which was ordered by the United States and Japan for study.

Because of the success of Junkers land-based aircraft, many of them were fitted with floats which allowed them to reach areas where there were no landing facilities.
This Junkers G.24.W, moored here in Copenhagen, was a case in point.

another 17 for use in other parts of the world; and five were built in Japan and went into service on the Tokyo-Shanghai route.

In a commercial role, the Wal distinguished itself carrying mail in the South Atlantic. Not having the colonial links of the French Aéropostale, D.L.H. set up the first express connection between Rio de Janeiro and Berlin in March 1930, using the Dornier as far as Fernando de Noronha just off the coast by Natal. There the mail was transferred onto a ship, the *Cap Arcona*, which went as far as Las Palmas. The mailbags were then flown to Berlin. With these various transshipments it took eleven days to transport an item of mail, until 1934 when the Dornier Wal *Monsun* took off from the ship *Westfalen* with the aid of a catapult which shot it into the air in two seconds.

On February 7th 1934, the Wal machines began a regular service, crossing the ocean at a height of only 30 feet in order to take advantage of the ground effect. This practice, which was exhausting for the pilots, allowed greater distances to be covered. Mail was carried from Germany to Brazil in four days. Six ten-ton Do J II Wal aircraft were bought for this route. The distance they could cover nonstop was increased at the cost of a slight reduction in speed.

By September 1939, 328 crossings of the South Atlantic had been made by D.L.H. as opposed to 428 by Air France, but all the German crossings were undertaken by the same machine – the Wal.

From 1926, Dornier offered the Do R Superwal, which was larger and more powerful than its predecessor and designed to take 19 passengers instead of 10. The twin-engined version, of which three were made, was used by D.L.H., while the four-engined version flew mainly in the colours of S.A.N.A., who bought six for use on Mediterranean routes, and of D.L.H., who used them in the Baltic. Two Superwal machines were bought by Stout in the United States, with accommodation for 29 passengers, to cover connections between the cities of Cleveland, Detroit and Chicago.

Just one manufacturer tried to compete with Dornier. This was Rohrbach, who offered the Ro V Rocco to D.L.H. This seaplane with all-metal construction carried 10 passengers, but after experimental operation for two months in 1928 the company turned it down. Rohrbach then offered the Romar, which was intended for transatlantic operation, but after tests beginning on August 7th it was discovered that the seaplane only had a range of 1,250 miles instead of twice that distance as had been specified. The three Romars were refitted for service on the Baltic, and a fourth went to St Raphael where it was assessed by the French Navy.

Servicing a Dornier Super Wal in a hangar at Friedrichshafen on Lake Constance.
D-1115 was in fact the first of the 17 Super Wal machines that were built, three with two engines and 14 with four.

Both the takeoff and the touchdown of the Dornier Do X were an amazing spectacle. Here the machine has twelve 610hp Curtiss Conqueror engines.

The twelve 525hp Siemens Jupiter engines caused numerous problems at the beginning of the Do X's career. They were replaced by Curtiss units in February 1930.

A MIGHTY GIANT

The Dornier Do X has a very special place in the history of flying boats. Strictly speaking, it was not a commercial aircraft, since it never went into service on a regular route, but by realizing the dream of a giant flying boat which Claudius Dornier had cherished since 1915 it became the standard-bearer for German marine aviation.

The project was being researched as early as 1919, but the design took seven years to reach completion in December 1926. The machine was jointly financed by the manufacturer and the German transport ministry, and built at Altenrhein on the Swiss part of Lake Constance, in order to escape the wrath of the Allied Commission. Construction began on December 19th 1927, and less than two years later, on July 12th 1929, the flying boat was launched.

The sight of the Do X staggered those who saw it. With a wingspan of 157ft 5ins, a length of 134ft 2ins and a height of 33 feet, the metal monster was driven by twelve 525hp Siemens Jupiter engines mounted in tandem. The hull with two steps had a sharply pointed nose. A rudder fitted at the end of the second step helped manoeuvring on the water. The huge stabilizer fins

August 27th 1931: the Do X flies over Manhattan and its skyscrapers.

The service on board the Do X was up to the standard of the transatlantic liners, even if the passengers were sometimes all asked to crowd together on one side to help the giant flying boat to make a turn.

followed the pattern that Dornier was so attached to. The machine was fitted out for carrying 66 passengers on long distances or about 100 over short hauls. A remarkable system enabled the mechanics to gain access to each engine unit from the wing surface. The crew of 14 were accommodated on the upper deck in front of the leading edge of the wing. The wings themselves were made up of a metal framework for the most part covered in fabric.

On July 12th 1929, just after launching, the pilot Richard Wagner managed to perform three short hops as he crossed the lake at high speed. On July 25th he had the monster airborne in 28 seconds with only eight engines, and flew over Lake Constance for 2½ minutes with 25 passengers on board. The first official flight took place on July 29th, when Claudius and Maurice

Dornier with 15 of their closest collaborators flew for an hour. The trials that followed went very well, the one initial difficulty being the distance required for takeoff. With a load of 48 tons, the Do X taxied for 65 seconds, but with 51½ tons it needed 130 seconds.

In ideal conditions, the Do X took off on October 21st with 150 passengers, a crew of 10 (and nine stowaways!). With this load of 48 tons, it took off in 50 seconds and climbed slowly to a height of 650 feet. After flying for 40 minutes at 105mph, it touched down on Lake Constance. The record that the aircraft had just set by carrying 169 passengers went on to stand for nearly 15 years.

The main problem with the Do X was the engines, which would not lift it to an altitude of more than 1,400 feet. After 103 flights, the last of which took place on February 14th 1930, the Do X returned to the factory to be fitted with water-cooled Curtiss Conqueror engines developing 610hp. On August 4th 1930, it took off and reached an altitude of 1,650 feet. After a total of 318 test flights, the results were considered satisfactory, and the Do X could cross the Atlantic.

Painted entirely in white, the Do X left its base on November 5th 1930, reaching first the Zuiderzee then Calshot, before touching down at Lisbon on November 27th. A series of incidents held up Captain Christiansen (the former fighter ace from the German navy), his crew and the few handpicked passengers.

On May 1st the enormous machine began its long tour following the coasts of Africa as far as the island of Bubaque, off the coast of Portuguese Guinea. On June 4th, after a false start, the Do X taxied for 4½ minutes before taking off with a load of 51 tons, including a crew of 13 and 5,520 gallons of petrol. The flight began at a speed of 112mph and an altitude of only 30 feet

to take advantage of the ground effect. At night the aircraft climbed to 80 feet as a safety measure. After flying for 13 hours under these very testing conditions, the giant touched down at Fernando de Noronha before dawn. 1,400 miles had been covered at a speed of 108mph. On June 5th it travelled the remaining 217 miles to Natal; it flew on to Rio de Janeiro on June 20th, staying there until August 5th when it turned north again. After numerous stops for celebrations, the Do X touched down in New York on August 27th. It took up its winter quarters at the Glenn H. Curtiss Airport, where the engines were completely overhauled.

On May 19th 1932, the Dornier left the American capital for Newfoundland. On May 21st the flying boat took off with a record load of 53.3 tons in less than two minutes, took up the ground effect position at 10 feet over the sea and flew in this manner for several hours, before climbing to 65 feet. By travelling like this for 1,550 miles, the crew accomplished a remarkable feat of piloting. In sight of the Azores, Christiansen decided to bring the machine down and, being short of fuel, it taxied to Horta using only four engines. After spending some time at Calshot, the Do X ended its grand tour on the Müggelsee near Berlin, where it was awaited by a crowd of 200,000. It then made a tour of the Baltic before returning to Lake Constance on November 14th 1933.

After an experimental assignment with D.L.H. lasting two months, it made its last flight in 1934 to Berlin where it was to be exhibited at the Air Museum.

Two further Do Xs were delivered to Italy. Driven by 550hp Fiat A.22R engines, Do X2 and X3 did not fulfil the S.A.N.A.'s criteria for commercial operation; they were handed over to the military, who used them for prestige flights. The first machine was eventually delivered on August 28th 1931 via the Alps: the necessary altitude of nearly 13,800 feet was achieved at a speed very close to stalling. The second machine arrived at La Spezia on May 13th 1932. Both were taken out of service in 1934. While having all the appearance of a dinosaur, inherently unviable because of its weight, the Do X fulfilled its experimental function perfectly

Although incapable of carrying a profitable load across the seas, it showed great robustness and longevity, which were essentially due to its metal construction. While away from its base for two years it was always in the open, without suffering any deterioration as a result.

It was due to men as enterprising and audacious as Claudius Dornier that marine aviation and aeronautics in general were able to progress. The Do X was no doubt a half-failure, but even so it remains one of the most remarkable seaplanes in history.

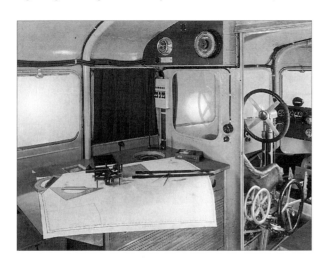

The chart room and cockpit of the Do X were situated on the upper deck.

The Dornier Wal installed on the catapult of the *Friesland*. It made reconnaissance flights in the North Atlantic in 1937.

The Dornier Wal D-AGAT is catapulted from the *Schwabenland* to start on a mail flight across the North Atlantic, barely skimming the waves.

ATTACKING THE NORTH ATLANTIC

To save time in the transportation of mail, the Germans experimented with using small float-planes catapulted from ocean liners, an experiment also tried out by the French Transatlantique company. The first aircraft to make a flight of this type was the Heinkel He 12, its journey beginning more than 300 miles out from New York on July 22nd 1929. The following year the Heinkel He 58 was also used for this kind of assignment. In 1932 these machines were replaced by Junkers Ju 46s. In all, 198 catapult launches were made over a period of seven years.

In 1936 a much more ambitious programme was set up. The

One of the most attractive flying boats ever made, the Dornier Do 18 was the first to use diesel engines, which were 600hp Jumo 205Cs. D-ANHR, which first flew on January 11th 1937, was the first Do 18F.

The successor of the Dornier
Wal in its general shape, the
aerodynamic qualities of the Do
18 were not enough to
compensate for the engines'
lack of power.

Dornier Do 18, which looked like a reprofiled Wal, flew for the first time on March 15th 1935. On September 11th the machine was launched by catapult off the Azores and reached New York after a flight of 22 hours. Using both the northern and the southern routes, *Zephir* and *Aeolus* covered 23,372 miles in 40 days and eight crossings, showing that it really was possible to create a new service.

The next year the Blohm und Voss Ha 139 took over. This was a very handsome four-engined float-plane, 64 feet long with a wingspan of 88ft 6ins and made its first flight in October 1936. Deutsche Lufthansa took delivery of two Ha 139s and a Ha 139B, which was a slightly larger version. They made 14 crossings in 1937, and 26 the following year. Catapult launching meant the saving of a ton and a half of fuel as compared with a normal takeoff.

In the South Atlantic, where they were also deployed, the Ha 139s did not need to resort to catapult launching, because they only had to cover a distance of 2,300 miles as compared with 3,100 miles in the North Atlantic. This aircraft had a cruising speed of 161mph as against the Do18's 115mph, and it carried 1,050lb of mail, as against the 660lb of the Dornier.

The Dornier Do 26, which was to replace it, made its first flight on May 21st 1938. It had four engines in tandem, and two were built for D.L.H. It crossed the South Atlantic 18 times before the declaration of war, and showed a significant improvement in speed, since it could reach a maximum of 208mph and maintain a cruising speed of 192mph.

The fears of the Allied Commission 20 years earlier proved to be justified, since the Do 18, Ha 139 and Do 26 acted as prototypes for military aircraft which took part in the war.

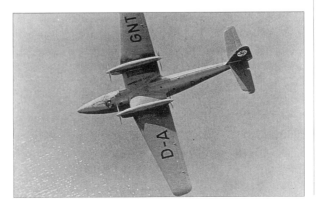

**The Dornier Do 26A was
designed to cover 5,600 miles
nonstop, so that it could fly in
perfect safety from Lisbon
to New York.**

For the first time retractable floats
in the wings replaced the
stabilizing fins, helping to give the
Do26A a 208mph top speed.

Without any doubt the craziest commercial flying boat ever to fly, Caproni's Triple Triplane was a monster intended to carry 60 passengers across the Atlantic.

The dream was shattered on March 4th 1921, when the machine did a nose dive into the waters of Lago Maggiore.

The Macchi MC.100 was used on the Rome-Cagliari-Barcelona-Lisbon route by Ala Littoria from 1939.

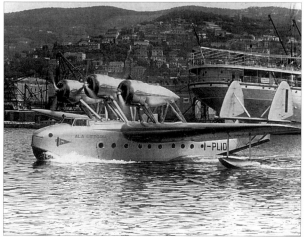

ITALIAN COMMERCIAL OPERATIONS

The Italians concentrated on solving the problems of flying in the Mediterranean. They started by developing military seaplanes which they adapted for passenger transport, such as the Macchi M.18 directly derived from the M.9 and used in the Adriatic. There followed numerous types produced by Macchi, Savoia or Cant. The most outrageous machine remains the Caproni Transaero Ca.60 Triple Triplane, one of the strangest flying machines in the history of aviation.

The Capronissimo

The Ca.60 was intended to cross the Atlantic with 60 passengers, or 100 on shorter journeys, or alternatively to carry 7½ tons of mail. Fitted with no less than eight 400hp Liberty engines, the triple triplane was a tailless aircraft, steered by means of the non-symmetrical use of the ailerons on the front and rear wings. In fact this monster was not only uncontrollable because the controls were so complicated, but also unstable on its three axes. In spite of this, the extraordinary machine began its tests on Lake Maggiore in February 1921. Two days later, the Ca.60 piloted by Semprini set off for its first flight. Its fuselage contained sandbags as the equivalent in ballast to 60 passengers. At an altitude of about 60 feet, the flying boat suddenly went into a nose dive and plunged into the water. The crew extracted themselves from the wreckage, and when the fuselage had been salvaged from the water it was discovered that the ballast had not been properly secured. In spite of Caproni's efforts to reconstruct the machine, the first Ca.60 was to have no successor as a fire put an end to the venture.

The adaptation of the Savoia-Marchetti S.55 for commercial operation did not present any particular problems, five or six passengers being accommodated in each hull. The S.55C and S.55P were put into service on the Brindisi-Istanbul and Rome-Cagliari routes. Their success did not stop there, since the American Aeronautical Corporation bought two for the United States. In 1932 a three-engined version known as the S.66 was introduced. Each hull could seat up to nine passengers.

Ala Littoria provided themselves with 16 Cant Z 506Cs powered by 800hp Alfa Romeo engines in 1936. This version achieved a speed of 236mph with cruising at 200mph and a range of 807 miles carrying 16 passengers. One Z 506C, registration I-ALAL, completed a flight from Rome to Buenos Aires and back at an average speed of 300kph (186.3mph) in March-April 1938.

During the war 11 further Z 506Cs were built, taking the total number of transport seaplanes to 38. In 1938 the all-metal Z 509, destined for transatlantic mail carrying, also set up new records. It had a cruising speed of 217mph, with a possible maximum of 280mph, and could cover distances of 2,110 miles, which made it a remarkable machine. Only three were made, and it was only used for military purposes.

The progress made by Italian transport seaplanes was astonishing. After the dream of the Capronissimo the constructors showed remarkable realism. The Italian airlines acquired the S.55, a military aircraft which they adapted to their needs, then thanks to the boldness of Filippo Zappata they developed and used the Cant Z.506, which was later converted into a bomber by the air force. This machine had qualities which made it perfect for air sea rescue, and it was used in this role until 1960, which represents exceptional longevity for an aircraft of this date.

The Cant Z.506, fitted with 760hp Wright Cyclone engines, operated on the Mediterranean routes in 1936.
Its speed was exceptional at the time for a floatplane.

Seen on its step on the point of liftoff, the Short S.23 *Canopus* was the first of the C class flying boats.
It flew for the first time on July 4th 1936, and was delivered to Imperial Airways on October 22nd of the same year.

BRITISH COMMERCIAL OPERATIONS

Because air connections with European capital cities did not necessitate the use of seaplanes, British commercial air transport developed in a variety of other directions.

In July 1919 the Supermarine Channel was the first machine licensed to carry passengers and in due course flying boats became truly indispensable for connecting the main cities of the British Empire. The preference was for coastal routes rather than long direct flights. The way to the Indies was opened up on March 30th 1929 by a Short S.8 Calcutta going from Genoa to Alexandria via Rome, Naples, Corfu and Athens. Five of these three-engined aircraft, carrying 15 passengers at 93mph, were built. The land route was already covered by conventional aircraft. London to Karachi took seven days, with an extension to reach Delhi. Three Short S.17 Kents replaced the Calcuttas from May 1931.

The route to South Africa called for the use of an S.8 for the section from Cairo to Mwanza on Lake Victoria. On the other hand, this flying boat was no use for Hong Kong or Australia.

Shorts for the Empire

In 1934, Imperial Airways first ordered two Short S.23s, then bought 26 on sight of the plans, which at the time was an unusual sign of confidence. The first example, named *Canopus*, was launched on July 2nd 1936 and flew the following day, piloted by John Parker. With a wingspan of 113ft 10ins and a length of 87ft 11ins, the all-metal S.23 had four 920hp Bristol Pegasus XC engines. It could carry 3½ tons of mail and 24 passengers at a speed of 174mph with a range of 775 miles. It was fitted out with two decks, the upper one housing the crew and the cargo, while the lower one had four cabins for the passengers, who were reduced to 16 in number on night flights. The machine weighed 10.6 tons empty and 18.4 tons fully laden. After particularly successful test flights, the *Canopus* arrived at Genoa on October 22nd and went into service with Imperial Airways on October 30th 1936 on the Brindisi-Alexandria route. The British saw this memorable event as a triumph for their commercial air fleet, the flying boats proving to be an undeniable improvement on land-based aircraft. Some outstanding flights

followed, with the *Caledonia* modified for longer flights in view of the establishment of a mail service on the North Atlantic route. On December 21st 1936 it crossed the Mediterranean from Alexandria to Marseilles nonstop in 11hrs 15mins, then on February 18th 1937 it covered the 2,217 miles between Southampton and Alexandria in 13hrs 5mins. It was particularly due to the S.23 that Imperial Airways succeeded in overcoming competition from the railways, especially by linking Southampton and Alexandria with just one stop at Brindisi, starting on January 12th 1937. The year 1937 saw a whole series of survey flights accomplished by these flying boats, which were being made at the rate of two per year. In May, the *Cavalier* made a flight from Bermuda to New York prior to starting a regular service, from June 16th 1937 to January 21st 1939, on which date it crashed after losing the use of two engines. From June to September the *Cambria* flew from Hythe to Lisbon and back, a run of more than 10½ hours. The *Caledonia* explored the North Atlantic via Newfoundland, then via Portugal and the Azores. The *Cordelia* left Karachi on November 15th for Singapore, which it reached

Trial in-flight refuelling of the Short S.30 *Cabot* by a Handley Page Harrow.
Imperial Airways, handicapped by the restricted range of the Short S.23 and S.30, was able to provide a transatlantic service by virtue of this technique.

The one and only Short S.20 *Mercury* could fly at up to 210mph.
It was intended to convey mail across the North Atlantic, after being launched from the S.21 *Maia*.

were killed in this accident. On October 1st 1937, the *Courtier* crashed into Phaleron Bay near Athens as a result of a navigational error caused by a mirage effect. The hull broke in two and three passengers were drowned. Finally on December 5th the *Cygnus* 'porpoised' in an uncontrollable manner when taking off at Brindisi, and then sank; two passengers were drowned. Subsequent tests showed that on a dead calm sea with the flaps lowered to the maximum extent, this flying boat lacked stability.

In 1938, the S.23s were named (not without reason) C class Empire flying boats. They provided a service to Egypt every day, to India four times a week, to East Africa three times a week, and to South Africa, Malaysia and Australia twice weekly.

Try anything once

Imperial Airways took an extraordinarily bold step to secure its position in the North Atlantic. Since the unladen weight of the S.23 penalized it over long distances, Captain R.H. Mayo, the airline's technical director, suggested to Short's in 1932 that they should study the idea of a composite. The research showed that this formula could produce some very promising results, and Short's started its construction in 1935. The lower machine was called the Short S.21 *Maia* and was a modified S.23 in which the chord of the wing was enlarged and the displacement of the hull increased. The fuselage had a mounting on top of it on which was placed the S.20 *Mercury*, a small float-plane with four 320hp Napier Rapier V engines. Capable of reaching a speed of 210mph, the S.20 weighed a maximum of 12.35 tons when launched and had a range of 3,875 miles in combination with the S.21. Its sole function was to carry mail.

The *Maia* flew for the first time on July 27th 1937, and the *Mercury* on September 5th. After a series of separate flights, the S.20 was installed on its mounting. The composite took off for the first time on January 20th 1938, and on February 6th the first separation was a complete success. Leaving Foynes in Ireland on July 21st 1938, the composite set course for Montreal, which the *Mercury* reached after 20hrs 20mins flying; Captain D.C.T. Bennett and A.J. Coster, who had been faced with headwinds of 30mph, still had 65 gallons of fuel left. The 550lb of mail was delivered in record time. After visiting New York, the machine returned to Britain under its own power via the Azores and Lisbon. The floats were then converted into fuel tanks, and the composite took off on October 6th with a maximum load of 12.35 tons for the *Maia*, the *Mercury* weighing in at just under 12 tons. On board were D.C.T. Bennett and I. Harvey, who established a straight-line distance record of 5,960 miles, touching down on the Orange River in South Africa after 42 hours flying.

on the 21st. Finally on December 3rd the *Centaurus* left Southampton for Australia and New Zealand. It arrived at Wellington on December 27th. The greatest successes of this year however came from the opening of new routes. On February 4th a regular service started in collaboration with Quantas linking Britain and Australia, the connection with Durban being created at the end of June by the *Centaurus*.

However, the success of the S.23 flying boats was tarnished in 1937 by three accidents. On March 24th the *Capricornus*, lost in a snowstorm, crashed into a mountain in the Beaujolais after a very short career of ten hours! The five members of the crew

Finally on November 29th and again on December 12th 1938, the composite was used to carry mail to Alexandria by night, but Imperial Airways gave up using it after that because of the prohibitive cost, which was uneconomic because of the relatively small load. So ended one of the strangest experiments in the history of civil aviation.

The British also tried out in-flight refuelling. Experiments had been made by military aircraft, but it had not been used operationally. Imperial Airways received the prototypes of the Armstrong-Whitworth AW.23 and the Handley-Page HP.51, which were converted into refuelling tenders. On January 20th 1938 the AW.23 transferred fuel to the S.23 *Cambria* for the first time. There followed a series of tests in all possible weather conditions, including fog. In spring 1939, three Handley-Page Harrow bombers were deployed at Gander and at Shannon to refuel the Short S.30s *Cabot* and *Caribou*. The S.30 had numerous improvements, including 1,010hp engines and a strengthened airframe.

On August 5th 1939 the regular weekly service from Southampton to New York in three stages started. Eight round trips were completed with the S.30s, necessitating 15 refuelling operations, which went perfectly. Only eight minutes were needed to transfer about 650 gallons of fuel. The war interrupted this service, which remains unique of its kind in the annals of commercial aviation.

Having first shown a marked lack of interest in marine aviation, the British entered the lists with flights over the seas then over the oceans to link Britain with the lands of the Empire,

The interior of the Short C class flying boats was particularly spacious, as is shown in this view of the promenade deck under the wings.

using a range of flying boats developed by Shorts. To compensate for an overweight structure that seriously reduced the range of the Short C class, the company came up with some very original solutions.

After the Second World War, during which they saw intensive service, a few C class aircraft resumed their peacetime role. It was thus that *Coriolanus* chalked up 18,500 flying hours before ending its career on December 20th 1947 as the last survivor still in active use.

The composite *Maia/Mercury* accomplished its first separation in flight on February 6th 1938.

After flying across the North Atlantic, the *Mercury* established a distance record on October 6th 1938 by covering 5,960 straight-line miles after being launched from the *Maia*.

The seaplane for the millionaire, the Loening Flying Yacht bristled with so many innovations that in 1921 its constructor received the highest distinction awarded by the American aircraft industry, the Collier Trophy.

COMMERCIAL OPERATION
IN THE UNITED STATES

The United States emerged from the First World War in an undeniably favourable position for the development of large flying boats capable of long-distance overseas flights. The fruitful collaboration between Curtiss and Porte had in fact enabled series production of the H-16 and F-5L, which the U.S. Navy were offering secondhand at very favourable prices, but it was up to companies to adapt the hulls for carrying passengers. Some businessmen took up the challenge, without much success, with the exception of I.M. Uppercu, who founded Aeromarine Airways with three F-5Ls. On November 1st 1919 this company inaugurated a service from Key West to Havana, hoping to take advantage of the rich clientele driven by prohibition to make forays into a country where there were no restrictions on the consumption of alcohol. A year later it received the first contract for delivering mail to foreign destinations; this new of turnover enabled them to carry on. On May 1st 1924 the non-renewal of the contract by the U.S. Mail brought the company's activities to an end. They had none the less carried more than 20,000 passengers without a single accident.

The American companies had the advantage of two proving grounds where seaplanes seemed to offer safer options than land-based aircraft: the Caribbean and the New York-Rio-Buenos Aires run. The Caribbean quickly became the takeoff point for Pan American Airways, founded on March 14th 1927, while the N.Y.R.B.A. Line, founded on March 17th 1929, scooped up a series of mail contracts with South American countries from Venezuela to Chile. This company was absorbed by Pan American on September 15th 1930.

Continuous expansion

Pan American Airways owed its success to the unwavering determination of its president, Juan Trippe, to make the American company the most famous in the world by offering a different service – routes linking the United States with the rest of the world, while the other American carriers of the day were solely preoccupied with developing a network of internal communications. Helped by solid financial support, Trippe acquired the aircraft best suited to his requirements, starting with the Sikorsky S-38. The prototype actually went into service in July 1928 with N.Y.R.B.A., and the first production example with Pan American in October. In all 38 'ugly ducklings' went into operation, initially to cover the Miami-Havana-Paramaribo-Panama-Belize-Miami route, but subsequently in all sectors including China..

The Commodore

The N.Y.R.B.A. under the management of Ralph O'Neill decided, on sight of the plans, to buy six Consolidated Model 16 Commodores, commercial derivatives of the XPY-1, a long-range bomber and patrol aircraft which the U.S. Navy had just ordered on an experimental basis. Fitted with two 575hp Pratt & Whitney Hornet engines, the Commodore made its first flight on October 1st 1929. It had to be able to carry 32 passengers over short distances, but to start with the accommodation was laid out for 22 passengers spread over several compartments..

Named *Buenos Aires*, the first Commodore went into service on December 23rd 1929. In February N.Y.R.B.A. inaugurated a mail service linking South America and the United States. Meanwhile the order was increased to 14 machines. In spite of a number of incidents the aircraft proved reliable, and Pan American continued to use them when it transformed N.Y.R.B.A. into Panair do Brasil. Redeployed in the Caribbean, the Commodores displayed unusual versatility for a flying boat of the period. Taken out of service in 1937, they were then sent to China or resold to civilian or military operators. The last machines in operation were to continue flying after the war, showing that the Commodore had been ahead of its time. It was the first of a long line of flying boats from Consolidated which ended with the Catalina.

Moored in Cuban waters, the Aeromarine Airways' Curtiss 75 *Ponce de Leon* proclaims on its sides: "Key West - Havana 75 minutes".
In the three years of its existence the company did not have a single accident.

The Consolidated Model 16 Commodore *Havana* was the third of a series of 14 machines ordered by N.Y.R.B.A.
The Commodore was one of a long line going from the Admiral to the Catalina.

The first Sikorsky S-40 flies over the industrial area of Bridgeport, Connecticut.

In appearance it was a scaled-up S.38.

THE FIRST CLIPPER

The technical and commercial success of the S-38 enabled Igor Sikorsky to take up the project of a large capacity aircraft again. Pan American was associated with the S-40 project, which turned out to be a scaled-up S-38. When he was shown it for the first time, Lindbergh expressed a certain disappointment at the designer's lack of bold thinking. At the sight of the network of struts and wires which supported and braced the wing, he ironically nicknamed the machine "the flying forest". He had his say, more seriously, in the choice between different technical options, such as the position of the pilot's cockpit. The company

ordered two S-40s in December 1929, and a third followed. The S-40's first flight took place on August 7th 1931. Like its predecessor, it had landing gear which simplified manoeuvring on the ground and made it possible to land on terra firma. For Basil Rowe, Pan American's chief pilot, "the S-40 has no bad habits, nor any particular fault".

In October 1931, the first S-40 was given the name *American Clipper*, after the great merchant ships which sailed to and fro across the oceans in the 19th century, carrying people and goods between America and the other continents. Fascinated by this great era which had ended with the disappearance of the sailing ship, Juan Trippe's ambition was to build up a fleet of aircraft to cross the oceans which would have the same kind of aura as the magnificent vessels of the last century. The S-40 was the first stage in this grand scheme.

The S-40 went into service on November 19th 1931 in the Caribbean. To give the event the maximum possible publicity, Lindbergh was at the controls as far as Baranquilla in Colombia. Designed to carry 38 passengers, the S-40 only took 16 in order to be able to transport a cargo of mail, which remained the main source of revenue for all the airlines. The three S-40s fulfilled their purpose.

In 1935 the landing gear was removed and 660hp engines were installed, with a change of designation to S-40A. These machines could take 40 passengers and provide a daily service from Miami to Havana and back. The advent of the DC-3 at the end of the thirties relegated the S-40As to freight transport, a task which they fulfilled until 1943 when they were finally scrapped.

Although not displaying any technical novelties, the Sikorsky S-40 was still an important aircraft because, by carrying a large number of passengers, it showed the direction in which the design offices should be working in order to produce an aircraft that was an economic proposition.

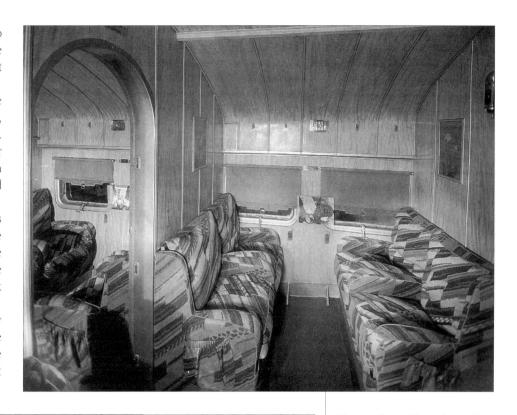

The comfort of the S-40's cabins is something travellers in today's aircraft can only dream of.

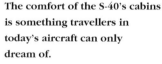

Passengers boarding the Sikorsky S-40 *Caribbean Clipper*. The S-40s were the first Pan American machines to carry the name Clipper.

The cargo of mail being loaded at the rear was absolutely indispensable for the profitability of the operation.

Arrival of the Sikorsky S-42B
Clipper III at Foynes, Ireland,
after a trial flight of 12hrs
40mins from Botwood,
Newfoundland,
on July 6th 1937.

The first Sikorsky S-42 went into service on the South American routes in August 1934.

This machine marked a very considerable advance over the S-40.

THE INVISIBLE REVOLUTION

Since the design of the S-40 was considered too conservative, Igor Sikorsky and his design office felt impelled to take risks with its successor. However, externally the S-42 did not display any features that were technically revolutionary, and for this reason it did not take the place in history that it deserved.

On October 1st 1932, Pan American ordered ten S-42s on sight of the plans, it being the practice at the time to work to a list of specifications required by a particular airline, without trying to go into series production. The company wanted a flying boat which could carry 32 passengers over a range of 1,000 miles. The S-42 flew for the first time on March 30th 1934, then set up ten world records before being delivered to its operator on June 5th.

The aircraft had four 700hp Pratt & Whitney Hornet engines fitted with automatic carburettors, a braced wing design with very heavy loading (the figure was not to be surpassed for another eight years by a transport aircraft), and very large flaps permitting reduced takeoff and landing speeds as well as distances. In addition, there was an extremely favourable relationship between the (carefully controlled) unladen weight and the payload. What is more, the S-42 which weighed just under 17 tons could cruise at 150mph, with a maximum of 186mph. Political problems prevented the S-42 from providing a regular mail service across the North Atlantic, so Pan American turned to the Pacific. The second S-42, with its seats removed and fitted with additional fuel tanks, had a range of 2,800 miles. Throughout 1935, it undertook survey flights on the route San Francisco-Honolulu-Midway-Wake-Guam-Manila. It arrived back at San Francisco on October 24th, and Pan American was granted the trans-Pacific mail contract. Four more powerful S-42As were delivered for the Latin American network; three were to remain in service until 1946. Three S-42Bs capable of operating over longer distances completed the Pacific route, which was inaugurated on December 23rd 1937, but the operation was stopped after the second regular flight because of the loss of the first S-42B. Ed Musick, Pan American's Chief Pilot, was killed in the accident, as well as his crew. The second S-42B covered the Manila-Hong Kong route, and the third machine alternated with the Short S.23 *Cavalier* on a mail service between Bermuda and New York or Baltimore, before undertaking a series of survey flights in the North Atlantic.

All the different versions of the S-42 played their part in the American war effort before being broken up in 1946.

The Martin M-130 *China Clipper* flies over the Baltimore docks during of a test flight.

CHINA CLIPPER

Unlike the Sikorsky S-42, the Martin M-130 had the advantage of an unusual amount of publicity. Proposed at the same time as its rival, three were ordered in 1933 for operation on the Atlantic routes. Unfavourable political conditions prevented the project from going ahead, so Pan American decided to switch the M-130 to the Pacific routes. This change greatly altered the requirements as the longest run, from San Francisco to Hanoi, was 17% longer than that from Newfoundland to Foynes. Allowing for headwinds and leaving a small safety margin, the possible payload was reduced to a disastrous extent.

When the M-130 *China Clipper* made its first flight, it was America's largest aircraft. It had a length of 90ft 7ins, a wingspan of 130ft and a gross weight of 23 tons. Its four 800hp Pratt & Whitney Twin Wasp engines gave it a maximum speed of 210mph with a cruising speed of 160mph. Carrying mail and freight, it had a range of 4,000 miles, and with 12 passengers 3,000 miles. Pan American's publicity proclaimed that it could carry 41 passengers and a crew of eight, which may be true, but nobody is saying over what distance!

The *China Clipper* inaugurated the San Francisco-Manila mail service on November 22nd to 29th 1935, returning on December 6th. Three aircraft were used in alternation from the beginning of the following year. On October 21st 1936 the commercial service was initiated by the *Hawaii Clipper*, and nine passengers alighted at Manila on October 27th. This was an important date in the history of aviation, since it was the first trans-oceanic service available to passengers.

The M-130 had such a powerful image that it co-starred with Pat O'Brien and Humphrey Bogart in a film made in 1936 called *China Clipper*.

On July 28th 1938 the *Hawaii Clipper* completely disappeared between Manila and Guam, causing the death of six passengers and the crew of nine. The *Philippine Clipper* escaped a bombardment at Wake, then reached Midway with 39 people on board just after the attack on Pearl Harbor on December 7th 1941. On January 21st 1943 the machine hit a mountain in California with 19 people on board. The *China Clipper* was added to the list of losses on January 8th 1945 when it sank at Port of Spain, in Trinidad. The death toll was 23, with seven survivors.

Having once made newspaper headlines around the world, the M-130 faded away to general indifference, its achievements no longer counting for anything very much compared with those of the military aircraft used at the end of the war to carry a clientele of V.I.P.s.

Because of the length of the Transpacific flights Martin installed Pullman-style couchettes in the cabin of the M-130.

A Hollywood view of air travel, the film *China Clipper* starred Pat O'Brien (left) and Humphrey Bogart (right), seen here at the controls of the Martin M-130.

BOEING IN THE ASCENDANCY

From 1935 onwards, Pan American was considering a successor for the S-42 and M-130. The choice went to Boeing, which was considered to be the second most important manufacturer, although the Sikorsky S-45 offered a better performance. Lindbergh expressed his dissatisfaction, but Juan Trippe wanted to have a genuinely transoceanic aircraft as quickly as possible. A contract for six Boeing Model 314s was signed in July 1936. The first example flew on June 7th 1938, nine months after the date

planned, but 10 months ahead of the delivery date given for the S-45. The machine used the wing design of the XB-15, as well as its engine nacelles and parts of its tail. Originally it only had one tail fin, but to the horror of Eddie Allen, who was at the controls for the aircraft's first flight, the Boeing 314 refused to turn. The pilot only succeeded in doing this by using the thrust of the engines. The problem was solved by fitting first two, then three tail fins.

The 314 received its certificate in January 1939, and went

The Boeing 314 *Atlantic Clipper* at liftoff on the second step, using all the power of its 1,500hp engines.

Over Puget Sound, the two most recent Boeing products in 1938, the Y1B-17A Flying Fortress and the first 314, *Honolulu Clipper*.

into service on March 29th on the San Francisco-Singapore run. It was the largest commercial aircraft of its day: with four 1,200hp Wright Double Cyclone engines it took off with a weight of 36½ tons and a maximum payload of 10,000lb, while it could reach a speed of 208mph and cruise at 183mph. Designed to carry 74 passengers, in fact it had difficulty transporting more than 25 on oceanic flights.

On May 20th 1939 the *Yankee Clipper* flew from Port Washington to Marseilles via the Azores and Lisbon in 29 hours with a ton of mail. On June 24th the same machine took the northern route to Southampton. The passenger service was finally inaugurated on June 28th by Captain R.O.D. Sullivan at the controls of the *Dixie Clipper*, with 22 passengers crossing the Atlantic to disembark at Marseilles. The price of the ticket ($375) represents twice the cost today of a one-way flight over the same route in Concorde - air travel remained the preserve of a very small number of privileged people. On July 8th the Boeing

Yankee Clipper carried 17 passengers on the northern route with one stop at Botwood (Gander) and one at Foynes (Shannon).

Twenty years lie between the first crossing of the North Atlantic by the Curtiss NC-4 and the opening of a regular service connecting the United States and Europe. Thanks to Pan American, the United States got there before Britain and France. The politically inspired desire to bring about the demise of the Aéropostale, as well as technical backwardness, had put France out of contention. In Britain, stirring efforts in using such unconventional solutions as the composites and in-flight refuelling had only showed the limitations of the Short S.23.

Juan Trippe's ambition to set up a worldwide network became a reality due to a policy of persevering with the development of flying boats which fulfilled his precise requirements. The four machines designed exclusively for Pan American all provided the required technical advances. The Boeing 314 was the last link in the chain.

Hawker Ospreys, fighter/reconnaissance aircraft carried on board British cruisers.

They are passing over the port of Alexandria.

The declaration of war forced Pan American to fall back on Lisbon, which had a twice weekly service. In September 1940, the *California Clipper* opened the Los Angeles-Auckland run. Six machines designated 314As went into service from April 1941, three of them with B.O.A.C., the new name of Imperial Airways. This new version, fitted with more powerful engines and larger fuel tanks, had a maximum speed and a range that were superior to the original version, five examples of which were subsequently uprated to 314As. In spite of intensive use, only one Boeing was lost during the whole war period. In the history of marine aviation, this machine marks at one and the same time the crowning achievement of a quarter of a century of constant efforts to produce an aircraft for commercial transoceanic travel, and the end of an era, since the reliability of engines was now such that the use of flying boats, which had such aerodynamic disadvantages, was no longer justified. The land-based aircraft was about to replace the seaplane for transport across the oceans.

FROM ONE WAR TO THE NEXT

At the end of the First World War, military seaplanes had four principal tasks: they provided aerial superiority, reconnaissance, torpedo-firing capability and patrols which could also attack submarines. Two further tasks were added in the course of the following 20 years: air sea rescue and transport. Progress made in the general evolution of aviation did not benefit civilian and military seaplanes to the same extent. Additionally the funds allocated to the navy were very thinly spread, since as well as the armament of traditional ships there was the cost of aircraft carriers and their equipment. As a result the development of military seaplanes remained dependent on that of civil machines.

The twenties were the decade of the Dornier Wal, which first flew in 1922. Bringing together the best of the ideas inherited from German research in the First World War, it was adopted by about a dozen countries for patrols over the open sea, torpedo-carrying and rescue work. Its metal construction and the use of lateral stabilizer fins gave it a considerable technical advantage, which were also of benefit to commercial operators. The Savoia S.55, which first flew in 1925, marked a definite break with the heritage of the war, at least in its shape. Capable of reaching 168mph, this torpedo aircraft had a performance comparable to that of its land-based competitors. Its configuration with twin floats (forming the fuselage) and twin booms, which was perfectly suited to its period, did not turn out to have much of a future. The successes of the thirties were versions of civil aircraft, such as the American Consolidated P2Y Ranger patrol aircraft, of

which 54 were built between 1932 and 1935, a direct derivative of the Commodore looking ahead to the Catalina. Others, such as the Cant Z.506B, were straight adaptations of civil seaplanes to a combat role. The Short S.25 Sunderland, another great success, belonged on the other hand to the generation designed from the outset for service in the Second World War.

Thus very few military seaplanes made a mark in the interwar period. This is clear from the meagre use the Spanish made of them in the Spanish Civil War.

The Consolidated XPY-1 Admiral, which first flew on January 10th 1929, was not adopted by the U.S. Navy.

The Cant Z.506B (a military bomber version) set up a world record by flying nonstop from Spain to Brazil in 1938.

The Second World War

THE DEVELOPMENT OF WATER-BASED AVIATION HAD REACHED ITS HIGH POINT IN THE THIRTIES, AND THE SECOND WORLD WAR WAS TO WITNESS ITS DECLINE. OF THE HUNDREDS OF THOUSANDS OF AIRCRAFT BUILT DURING THE WAR, ONLY TEN THOUSAND WERE SEAPLANES. UNABLE TO OFFER EFFECTIVE RESISTANCE AGAINST FIGHTER AIRCRAFT, THEY WERE RELEGATED TO ANCILLARY TASKS.

A formation of Chance Vought OS2U-2s on patrol in the Pacific.

The Dornier Do 24 represented the end of the line that had begun with the Wal, characterized by a high wing and lateral fins or sponsons.

At the start of the Second World War, the fleets of seaplanes in service with the main protagonists demonstrated at the same time the technical progress made by each country and the lack of interest in the development of the seaplane.

From October 1st 1933, Germany started to rearm, and created a naval air squadron at Warnemünde equipped with Heinkel He 60 floatplanes. Its strength was augmented by the introduction of Heinkel HD38 and He 51w single-engined single-seater fighters, Heinkel He 60 spotter-reconnaissance machines, multipurpose Dornier Do 18s and He 59s, and Dornier Do 15s, the latest version of the Wal for maritime surveillance.

The growth of the German naval air arm remained below the forecast level because of a significant conflict of interest between the Kriegsmarine and the Luftwaffe, which wanted to have all military aircraft under its control.

In September 1938, due to the influence of Hermann

The Heinkel He 114A-2 was replaced as quickly as possible by the Arado Ar 196, since its behaviour both on the water and in the air left so much to be desired.

Goering, the Kriegsmarine only had 63 Do 18s, 32 He 59s and 81 He 60s as its front-line seaplanes. The He 60 had been converted into a patrol aircraft, since its maximum speed of 150mph (lower than that of the Dornier Do 18) made it unusable as a fighter. It was therefore carried on board ships, from which it was catapulted.

In September 1939, at the beginning of the Polish campaign, the German Navy got rid of its few Heinkel He 114s, which had been intended to replace the He 60. Their mediocre performance both on the water and in the air made them useless.

In France, the naval air arm had a particularly heterogeneous collection of machines. The first bomber flotilla consisted solely of Lioré et Olivier LeO H.257 bis, six-seater torpedo bombers which first flew in 1934 as a naval adaptation of an airframe designed in 1929. The 35 examples of the H.257 bis in service,

with their maximum speed of 137mph and cruising speed of 112mph, seemed to belong to another age. In spite of its more modern appearance, the Latécoère 298, used for light torpedo duties, had such a modest performance – its maximum speed was 183mph – that the aircraft's crew could only rely on its manoeuvrability to have any chance of escape in case of attack. At the outbreak of war, 41 of these machines had been delivered, 35 of which belonged to the torpedo squadrons. For reconnaissance, 31 Breguet Bizertes, a military derivative of the Short Calcutta, were distributed over four squadrons; the others had four Latécoère 302s, three Latécoère 523s, six Loire 70s, and one Potez-CAMS 141.

The Laté 302s based at Dakar were the military version of the Croix du Sud of tragic memory; they were deployed to keep a watch on shipping along the coast of French Equatorial Africa. Apart from a range which allowed it to cover nearly 1,500 miles, which was very useful on missions that could last 16 hours, this ancient four-engined aircraft simply suffered from the climate and from corrosion.

The Laté 523, with a maximum takeoff weight of 42 tons, was the largest French aircraft. Fitted with six 920hp Hispano-Suiza 12y-27 engines, it was capable of remaining airborne for more than 20 hours at a speed of 115mph. It was also remarkably well suited to anti-submarine operations and to long-distance reconnaissance. What is more, crews appreciated the comfortable conditions in which their missions could be carried out. However the engines' lack of reliability, a maximum speed of 155mph and a ceiling for cruising that was much too low limited the number of operations that could be performed with this aircraft in the North Atlantic.

The six Loire 70s were deployed in the Mediterranean. Equipped with six 740hp Gnome-Rhône 9Kfr engines, they had been built to a 1931 specification using an outdated configuration and principles of construction, as was the case with all the French seaplanes in service in 1939. Its performance was ten years behind, with a maximum speed restricted to 143mph. Maintaining these machines required remarkable feats from the mechanics, if the Loire 70s were to be flown intensively. Their task from the very first day of the war was to keep watch on the Straits of Messina.

The sole Potez-CAMS 141, which flew for the first time in January 1938, was the only machine that offered a performance comparable to that of British, American or Japanese seaplanes. Although fitted with less powerful engines (920hp 12y-26/27s), its maximum speed of 202mph and its endurance of 30 hours enabled it to undertake long-distance reconnaissance in the North Atlantic.

The seven Loire 70s were assigned to the E7 squadron based at Karouba.
Four of these were still operational on June 12th 1940 when the Italians bombed the town. Only one survived the attack.

This wide assortment of aircraft posed enormous logistical problems, which were however lessened by the intensive use of the Breguet 521 Bizerte. The choice of this British three-engined biplane was a result of the inability of the French aircraft industry to series produce a flying boat for maritime patrols.

There were no fewer than eight different models in the reconnaissance category. The seaplanes chosen for these missions had the special feature that they could be catapulted from escort vessels, cruisers or battleships; they were also assigned to land-based squadrons. The force comprised two CAMS 37s designed in 1925 and 62 CAMS 37-11s with dual controls. The twin-engined CAMS 55, which was twice as heavy, could reach 133mph as against the 37-11's 118mph, again outdated levels of performance. The 34 CAMS 55s were in the process of being replaced by Loire 130s. The naval air arm also had 53 Gourdou-Leseurre GL810 to 812s, three-seaters which were even slower; 12 GL832s, slightly improved; 10 Potez 452s, which were also built to a 1930 specification, and 19 Levasseur P.L.14 and P.L.15 torpedo-carrying seaplanes.

This miscellaneous collection of machines was to be replaced by the Loire 130, of which 65 had already been delivered. Although not brilliant – the Loire 130 could fly at 140mph for five hours after a catapult launch or for seven hours taking off from the coast – it was a genuinely multipurpose aircraft since it could drop 150lb bombs and accommodate four passengers in addition to the crew of three on rescue missions. Its robustness made it a machine that could be operated without any problems far from its base.

In September 1939, France had – for another two months – the Loire 210, a fighter seaplane with catapult launching ability.

The 21 examples deployed with training squadrons, one of which was operational, had a very disappointing performance for a fighter plane with a top speed of 195mph. Moreover, serious structural problems resulted in the loss of a quarter of this force between August 10th and November 22nd 1939, so the machine was declared obsolete before it had had a chance to play any part in the Battle of France.

Great Britain was in a rather paradoxical situation, since the Royal Air Force, which was responsible for the defence of the coasts and maritime reconnaissance, had more combat seaplanes (in Coastal Command) than the Royal Navy, which had preferred to equip itself with aircraft carriers carrying biplanes with conventional undercarriages. Among the few seaplanes in its possession the most important was the Supermarine Walrus,

From the start of the German rearmament effort, a large number of seaplanes of different types passed through the Peenemünde test centre on the Baltic.
Beyond the Junkers Ju 52/3M is a Heinkel He 59B-2.

The Fairey Swordfish, although an old design, recorded some remarkable successes.
On April 13th 1940, catapulted from *H.M.S. Warspite*, one of these machines directed the gunfire which sank seven destroyers before itself destroying the submarine U-64.

descended from a long line starting with the Sea King and the Sea Lion of 1919, which took part in the Schneider Trophy and saw further development as the Seagull of 1922. The Walrus first flew in 1933 and went into service with the Fleet Air Arm three years later. A shipboard biplane suitable for catapult launching, the Walrus carried a pilot and two gunners, and was a multipurpose amphibian flying boat comparable to the Loire 130 and capable of 137mph. At the beginning of the war it was serving as part of 26 shipboard flights on cruisers, and on board the seaplane carrier *H.M.S. Albatross,* to which 710 Squadron was attached, with a complement of six Walruses. A total of 56 Walruses were in service in 1939.

The Fleet Air Arm also deployed some floatplanes, either designed as such from the start such as the Fairey Seafox, or adapted from aircraft with conventional undercarriages such as the Fairey Swordfish. The Seafox was a light reconnaissance biplane with catapult launching ability, carried on cruisers. Its top speed was less than 125mph. Five catapult flights and two training squadrons were equipped with Seafoxes.

The Fairey Swordfish in its seaplane version was a conventional biplane, without any particular vices, but outdated with its maximum speed of 134mph and its inability to climb to 10,000 feet in less than 14 minutes. It carried a load of 1,500lb-1,600lb, comprising either a torpedo or a mine or bombs.

Swordfish seaplanes made up the strength of three catapult flights.

All the catapult flights distributed among the Royal Navy's warships were brought together in January 1940 to form a single unit, 700 Squadron, which then had 42 Walruses, 11 Seafoxes and 12 Swordfish.

Since the Fleet Air Arm's task was only the protection of the fleet, the R.A.F. through the agency of Coastal Command concerned itself with the protection of the coasts, maritime reconnaissance and anti-submarine warfare. For these missions it had at its disposal ten squadrons of Avro Anson 1s and three of Lockheed Hudson 1s, amounting to more than 200 operational landplanes as against 55 seaplanes, made up of two Saro Lerwicks, 17 Saro London IIs, nine Supermarine Stranraers and 27 Short Sunderland 1s.

The Saro London II was a twin-engined metal biplane with twin tail fins, which could carry a varied load of 4,070lb on missions lasting five hours. Its 920hp Pegasus engines allowed it to reach 150mph, a higher speed than the British shipboard seaplanes. The 23 London IIs served in 201, 202, 204 and 240 Squadrons.

The Supermarine Stranraer was the same type of machine as the London II. It is surprising to note that its designer, R.J. Mitchell, was also the originator of the Supermarine seaplanes that won the Schneider Trophy and of the legendary Spitfire. However that may be, 209 Squadron was equipped with nine Stranraers. This aircraft's strong points were an endurance of more than nine hours and a maximum speed of 165mph.

The Short Sunderland may be considered the only modern British seaplane in service at the declaration of war. It was a development of the Short C class Empire flying boat for military purposes, and of all the seaplanes made during the Second World War it remains unique as a military seaplane in series production (739 units) which was based on the airframe of a commercial seaplane, itself made in large numbers. We will return to this interesting machine in more detail later. Suffice to say here that it could reach 210mph, cruise at 175mph and go on patrol for more than 10 hours at a stretch. On September 3rd 1939 the 35 Sunderlands were distributed among 204, 210, 228 and 240 Squadrons.

The Saro Lerwick, which began to replace the London IIs in No.240 Squadron, had been provided in order to augment Coastal Command's force with a twin-engined aircraft less weighty than the Sunderland. It turned out to be very disappointing. At cruising speed its nose constantly described figures of eight (going into a Dutch roll), its takeoff performance was very poor, and in some situations it would stall viciously, all of which pilots were to learn to their cost. However only two examples were delivered to 240 Squadron.

In all the air forces preparing to confront one another in Europe, seaplanes had been particularly neglected with regard to both quality and to quantity. With the exception of the Dornier Do 18 in Germany, the sole CAMS 141 in France and the Short Sunderland in Britain, none of the machines in active service could stand comparison with their landplane equivalents. Quantitatively, it is obvious that the priorities were elsewhere, as can be seen from the case of the R.A.F.: out of 5,165 first-line machines, 75 were seaplanes, of which only 35 displayed any real efficiency. The ratio was slightly more favourable in Germany, since out of 3,162 operational machines in the Luftwaffe and the Kriegsmarine 150 were seaplanes.

However, in spite of this very unfavourable situation, seaplanes were to prove that they still had a vital part to play in the war in the air.

A Gourdu-Leseurre GL 812 being catapult-launched.
With a maximum speed of only 112mph, this seaplane was completely outdated by the beginning of the war.

The Dornier Do 26 was designed for the Lisbon-New York run carrying a cargo of mail.
In military form, it was first used in Norway, after which the three survivors maintained lines of communication.

The Loire 130 was the sole success among French seaplanes.
Having served as a multipurpose seaplane for catapult launching, in November 1942 it was transferred to coastal surveillance duties. It continued to serve in the naval air arm until 1950.

FIRST ENCOUNTERS

In spite of being so few in number, German and British seaplanes soon found themselves in the thick of the fighting. Coastal Command started its reconnaissance in the North Sea on August 24th 1939, three days after the *Graf Spee* had left Wilhemshaven. When war was declared, two Londons were on patrol in the North Sea, and the deadly cat and mouse game started officially. From August 26th, Dornier Do 18Ds made daily reconnaissance sorties.

The German naval air forces contributed to the Polish campaign launched on September 1st 1939, but only 61 seaplanes kept watch on the naval bases in the Baltic. On September 3rd, the minesweeper *Gryf* was sunk as a result of an attack by nine Heinkel 59Bs. The next day the same machines attacked coastal batteries and the liner *Schleswig-Holstein* in the port of Danzig. Their acts of aggression were broken off for fear that the British fleet would intervene in support of the Poles. On the Western Front on September 4th, a Blenheim tried to attack a Do 18D off Borken. The British aircraft was shot down by an enemy fighter which was protecting the flying boat from possible attackers. The next day a Heinkel 115A which belonged to the 1 KFGr (Küstenfliegergruppe, coastal air force group) 106 – as did the Do 18D – shot down an Avro Anson on patrol in the North Sea. The pilot, although seriously wounded, was rescued by his attackers and taken prisoner. The same day a Do 18D responded to attack a Lockheed Hudson, but the two aircraft broke off the engagement without any serious damage. On September 12th it was the same story, but the crew of the Do 18D (possibly the same one) was picked up by a German U-boat. On the same day

near Norderney, the first confrontation between seaplanes took place. A Dutch Fokker T VIII W/G, which was a large torpedo-carrying floatplane, was fired on by a Heinkel 115A. Completely disregarding international conventions, it had taken as its target an aircraft from a neutral country.

On September 18th, the Germans launched a large-scale operation to find a British naval squadron which had left Scapa Flow. A total of 32 He 115As and Do 18Ds scoured the English Channel and the North Sea, without success. But on September 26th a Do 18D spotted the aircraft carrier *H.M.S. Ark Royal*, the battleships *H.M.S. Rodney* and *H.M.S. Nelson*, and their escort vessels, north of the Great Fisher Bank. The flying boat had time to radio their position before being intercepted. Although carried out with all the seaplanes available from Küstenfliegergruppen 106, 306 and 406 as well as two Luftwaffe units, the German attack based on the information provided proved to be ineffective.

On September 29th, a Do 18D from the 2 KFGr 506 escaped with some damage from the machine guns of a Hudson. In all, 13 seaplanes from the various services were destroyed by the Allies in the first month of the war.

On the French side, the reconnaissance squadrons began their missions off the coast of Brittany, the 2S1 being equipped with Gourdou-Leseurre GL812s and CAMS 55s; the 2S4 with GL 812s and CAMS 37-11s; the E6 with its three Laté 523s and the E8 with the one and only Potez-CAMS 141. On September 6th the Laté 523 Algol sighted a U-boat, but did not succeed in attacking it before it dived. On September 12th its bombs missed their target. The Potez-CAMS 141, still in its testing phase, only undertook one wartime mission. On their most exposed flank, the French Navy's seaplanes made little show of strength.

In the Mediterranean, which was so important for traffic with North Africa, a CAMS 55 of the 3S4 identified a U-boat off the

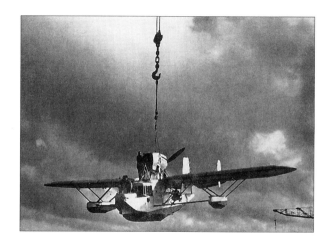

Cap d'Agde, but it did not have time to attack it; the next day three Gourdou-Leseurres had no better luck when confronted with another German U-boat. The only losses suffered were due to accidents.

Some sideshows

Operations in the North Sea intensified because Germany wanted to cut off the links between Scandinavia and Britain, while also protecting its copper route. On October 9th some Do 18Ds and He 115As came on a large naval squadron including two battleships. The Luftwaffe brought up 150 bombers, which did not manage to sink a single ship. Sea engagements required specialized aircrews and the right machines, which the Heinkel He 115 was not, as its defensive armament proved to be inadequate. Thus on October 21st nine of these aircraft with orders to attack a convoy ran into anti-aircraft fire and British fighters, which shot down four of them.

From mid-November onwards, German seaplanes were given a new task: the laying of magnetic mines. The big He 59B biplanes made their first missions, co-ordinated with those of the U-boats. This kept a number of He 59Bs and He 115As busy until December 7th, when the cold became too intense on the coast of the British Isles. About 30 machines were employed in the dropping of mines, but only a little more than half of these succeeded in completing their mission, the main objective being the Thames. In three months 250,000 tons of merchant shipping were sunk by this method.

Due to progress in radio communication, British shipboard seaplanes also introduced an innovation by providing information to the gunners after each salvo had been fired, so that the next one could be adjusted. The battleship *Graf Spee*, with which Coastal Command had lost contact, was eventually found in the South Atlantic off Montevideo. The Battle of the River Plate began on December 13th 1939 when German shells damaged two Walruses, which had to be jettisoned from *H.M.S. Exeter*. After being hit, the German battleship took refuge in the Uruguayan port. A Fairey Seafox was catapulted from the cruiser *H.M.S. Ajax* so that it could direct gunfire until the ship was destroyed. The Seafox, which was the Royal Navy's last float seaplane in a combat role, also went down in aviation history as the first machine to act as a gunlayer in a Second World War naval battle.

At the end of 1939, the combatants became increasingly interested in the strategic importance of Norway. Iron ore from Swedish mines was exported from Narvik, and was indispensable for both the German and Allied war effort. In November Finland's neutrality was violated by the U.S.S.R. On the 29th Do

18Ds began an attack on an important convoy. Out of 17 Dorniers involved, one machine was posted missing and four came down in the water in neutral or enemy territory. It must be noted that the climatic conditions were appalling and made any aerial operations hazardous, a reminder that seaplanes were not equipped to carry out missions in any weather. Winter put a stop to the missions, which were resumed in March 1940.

On March 12th and 17th Heinkel 115s tried without success to torpedo some ships. During the attack on 10 escorted cargo ships, two Do 18Ds had to alight on the open sea. At the beginning of April, an He 115B in trouble came down in the sea on the north side of the English Channel. The flight commander alighted to pick up the crew and to destroy the stricken Heinkel with the 15mm cannon fitted in the nose of the aircraft. On April 3rd two further Heinkels were lost. German seaplanes were suffering excessively heavy losses, a consequence of their use on inappropriate missions. On the other hand, they were displaying a formidable efficiency in minelaying, which was resumed in April in the Thames estuary, then extended to the French ports of Dunkirk, Boulogne and Calais from May 3rd.

The so-called "Weserübung" (Weser exercise), whose real aim was the invasion of Denmark and Norway, gave the seaplanes the new task of carrying troops and cargo. This task was to be allocated to three types of machine: firstly to landplanes fitted with floats, such as the Junkers Ju 52/3m W,

A Fairey Swordfish has just been catapulted from *H.M.S. Malaya*.

secondly to seaplanes such as the Heinkel 59B, which would be converted into transports. Thirdly machines would be used that had been designed for passenger transport, such as the Dornier Do 26, or originally for freight transport, such as the Blohm und Voss Ha 139B.

The seaplanes showed themselves to be perfectly suited to the Norwegian campaign. They put down commando units specially trained for mountainous terrain a long way up fjords which could only be reached from the sea. These commando units then created landing strips. The operation started on April 9th 1940. The units I, II and III KGz.b.v.108 See were equipped with 22 He 59Bs, two Blohm und Voss 138A-1s, three Ha 139Bs, two Do 24 prototypes and some Ju 52/3mg5e (See). The campaign quickly turned to the Germans' advantage. The British and French troops, lacking air cover, were forced onto the defensive, while the Sunderlands watched developments. One Allied machine disappeared on an impossible mission, which involved flying over the already occupied Stavanger and crossing

150 miles of mountainous country to reach Oslo, where it had to locate ships in the neighbouring fjords.

The seaplane transports recorded many interesting exploits on the run from Travemünde to Narvik, such as those of the two Do 26s on April 15th. The two Do 24 prototypes revealed the great qualities of this machine, which had lain forgotten at the Travemünde research centre. The Norwegian campaign rescued it from oblivion, and it became one of the great successes of marine aviation. Even so, the operations carried out by these machines involved considerable risks. On May 8th two Do 26s were attacked by R.A.F. Hurricane fighters just as they were about to put down commando units in the Rombaksfjord near Narvik, where the Allied troops were still putting up some resistance. One Dornier was shot down, and the other made a crash-landing in the water. The Norwegians captured its crew and the 10 soldiers it was carrying.

Allied troops evacuated Narvik on June 8th after destroying all the harbour installations.

The Heinkel He 115B-1 performed convoy escort duties in Norway.
Altogether 138 production examples were used by the German forces.

A survivor from another age, the Lioré et Olivier H.258 seems to have got into the wrong war, and is a perfect example of the backwardness of the French aircraft industry.

It was the only heavy bomber seaplane in the naval air arm.

THE BATTLE OF FRANCE

When the major offensive on the Western front began, the Kriegsmarine had 177 seaplanes at its disposal, of which 110 were operational.

On the French side, apart from the entry into service of the Lioré et Olivier H.43 as a replacement for the Loire 210 and doubling the number of Laté 298s, the naval air force had done nothing to develop its fleet of seaplanes nor had it tried to standardize those on its strength. The landplane forces on the other hand had been strengthened with the advent of machines better suited to modern warfare; this was a wise choice, since the seaplanes were to find themselves relegated to a subordinate role during the turmoil of May-June 1940.

On May 10th 1940, 12 He 59Bs took off from Zwischenahn Lake and landed at the two ends of the Willems Bridge over the Maas in the centre of Rotterdam. Shock troops disembarked and took control of the bridge, then of the Leeuwen and Jan Kuiten bridges. The surprise attack worked perfectly.

Of all the available French seaplanes, only one type saw any real action. This was the Latécoère 298, a distant relative of the Laté 290, which first flew in 1931. The Laté 298 took off for the first time on May 8th 1936. With a wingspan of 50ft 10ins and a length of 41ft 2ins, it was fitted with an 880hp Hispano-Suiza 12 Ycrs 1 engine which gave it a cruising speed of 155mph and a maximum of about 185mph in level flight. Depending on the particular version, it carried a crew of three or four. On May 10th 1940 about 60 were serving in operational units, 21 of them at Cherbourg and Boulogne. Lacking any naval targets suited to their main purpose as torpedo aircraft, the Laté 298s were thrown into the land battle from May 21st onwards.

The Laté 298s of the T2 flight made an armed reconnaissance over the ports of the Somme. Above Dieppe one of them tried to shoot down one of the Heinkel He 111s which were bombing the town, but the German aircraft was much too fast for its attacker, having a speed advantage of at least 60mph. The armed reconnaissance sorties did not produce any result against the enemy forces on the ground. On the other hand, two of the machines were slightly damaged by anti-aircraft fire. On the same day the six machines from T3 deployed at Boulogne left the town under bombs being dropped by the Luftwaffe, and managed to return to Cherbourg with some difficulty.

Four days later, four Laté 298s of the T2 flight given the task

A Laté 298 in Vichy colours flies over oil storage tanks at Dakar.

of bombing an armoured column were easy prey for nine Messerschmidt Bf 109Es. The robust construction of the torpedo aircraft meant that the pilots were able land two of them on the water off Boulogne and one at Cherbourg. The fourth came down on the ground, and the two survivors from the crew were taken prisoner. Three gunners were killed and one seriously wounded, which attested to the accuracy of the German gunfire. Shortly after, four Laté 298s attacked a fort near Boulogne. Their attack seemed crowned with success – until it was discovered that the fort was not under siege.

On May 23rd flight T3 was busy. Six Laté 298s received orders to attack enemy concentrations around Boulogne. The German flak hit one machine, which alighted on the sea without damage, its crew being picked up safe and sound by a French boat. The flight commander managed to put down at Cherbourg. The four remaining torpedo aircraft attacked Noyelles bridge without hitting it, and damaged the railway. In defence of the crews it must be said that the Laté 298 had been designed for launching a heavy torpedo in level flight, and its particular equipment was unsuitable for use in dive-bombing, which was the method for attacking this kind of objective. A further mission carried out by one seaplane from T2 and two from T3 with the aim of bombing this bridge, which was undefended, also failed.

A surveillance flight, the 1S1, was also given Laté 298s. Two machines made an armed reconnaissance sortie near Berck, without success. The next day, May 23rd, one of these torpedo aircraft was given the task of carrying mail into Dunkirk, which was under siege. The machine was surprised by a Messerschmitt Bf 110C and plunged into the sea. The gravely wounded pilot drowned in spite of the efforts of his radio operator, who was himself picked up by a French ship.

T3's Laté 298s took part in the fighting during the French campaign, but had little to show for it in spite of great courage on the part of the aircrews and senseless losses.

This day's toll was appalling: four aircraft destroyed, four dead, three wounded and two taken prisoner, with nothing to show in return. On the following days the Laté 298s contented themselves with maintaining a mail link with Britain, carrying out reconnaissance operations and escorting shipping. On the night of June 6th, three machines from T2 resumed their missions against armoured units near Abbeville. T3 sent three aircraft on June 9th to destroy the Noyelles bridge. Only one aircraft managed to identify its objective in the dark and attack it; the two others got lost, one of them never returning to Cherbourg and its two crew members being posted missing.

The next day, three LeO H 257 bis from B2 attacked the bridges on the Somme Canal in the dark, the operation being repeated on June 15th without suffering any loss. These large biplanes belonging to the same category as the Heinkel 51B were the only French seaplanes apart from the Laté 298s to have been in action during the invasion.

On June 10th, a Laté from T2 was brought down by French anti-aircraft fire; the crew was fortunately rescued. Two days later, two machines from the same flight bombed two U-boats which had just dived. Could the big patch of oil that resulted simply be a ruse on the part of the enemy in order to escape? However that may be, this was to be the one and only occasion when the Laté 298s were used to carry out their intended role of attacking shipping.

Italy's entry into the war on June 9th meant that the T3 flight had to join T4 based at Berre. The overflying of occupied France in a seaplane was a risky business. One machine crashed and a second made a crash-landing on the Garonne.

On the night of the June 17th to 18th eight aircraft belonging to these two flights bombed Finale Ligure, without suffering any losses. The next day T2 also undertook the trip down to Berre, with fatal consequences for one aircraft and its crew. On June

21st the seaplanes set off for Bejaia in Algeria. On the way they attacked a submarine, but their small 300lb bombs were ineffective, even when they actually exploded.

The hope that resistance could be kept up from North Africa disappeared with the signing of the Armistice on June 25th. In spite of the sacrifices shown by the aircrews which took them into action, French seaplanes only played a minor role during the invasion, being outclassed by their landplane opponents.

The conflict developed with the strengthening of the Axis powers. Italy threatened the British Empire in Africa and the Middle East. The British had to face the Luftwaffe during the Battle of Britain (July-September 1940) and then the Blitz (September 1940-June 1941), while fighting the Battle of the Atlantic from June 1940 onwards.

With the increase in the number of theatres of war, seaplanes were deployed on several fronts and some of them distinguished themselves. They were used particularly in the English Channel, not only for reconnaissance but also for rescuing aircrews, and in the Atlantic where the Short Sunderlands were the only aircraft that could provide air cover more than 300 miles out to sea.

The Laté 298 torpedo bomber was not effective in operation.

The Heinkel 59s which had served in the Spanish Civil War were used to fly commando units during the invasion of Holland, among other missions.

The Short Sunderland Mk 1 L2163 was the sixth to be built. It belonged to 210 Squadron. In this picture the rear hatch on the port side can be clearly seen.

THE SUNDERLAND

In 1935 Imperial Airways ordered 28 Short C class Empire flying boats on sight of the plans. The Air Ministry followed their example and bought 21 Sunderlands, this being the military version. It was the R.A.F.'s first monoplane four-engined flying boat. The prototype made its maiden flight on October 16th 1937, and the first examples entered service with 230 Squadron based at Singapore and 210 at Pembroke Dock. The Sunderland's

These two Sunderlands of 230 Squadron took part in the evacuation of Greece by British troops in April 1941. This mission showed the advantages of the flying boat on rescue missions.

1,010hp Bristol Pegasus XXII engines were mounted in wings with a span of 112ft 9fiins, while the length was 85ft 4ins. The crew of seven was spread out over the two decks, and enjoyed a certain degree of comfort with six bunks, a galley, and indeed everything necessary for flights of more than 10 hours. It could be armed with bombs and depth charges to a weight of 2,000lb. Its defensive armament was particularly impressive, and the Germans gave the aircraft the nickname "the flying porcupine". It was made up of eight 7.7mm machine guns, two in a Fraser-Nash turret in the nose, four at the rear, and two manual guns firing from the upper deck aft of the wings.

The Sunderland Mk 1 was used from the very first day of the war. On September 8th two German U-boats were bombed, but without any decisive result. The suitability of the large flying boat for unexpected emergencies was demonstrated on September 18th when three Sunderlands of 228 Squadron received SOS signals from a British cargo ship which had just been torpedoed. The pilot of the first aircraft spotted the wreck and 34 sailors squeezed into one open boat. A second Sunderland arrived on the scene to provide cover, while the other alighted close to the shipwrecked men, who were ferried to the flying boat in its two rubber dinghies. The Sunderland took off from the open sea with 21 survivors, and the second picked up the remaining 13.

Although overloaded, the two flying boats returned to touch down without any problems back at their base. This exploit – quite rightly acclaimed by the British propaganda machine – mapped out a new future role for the flying boats: rescue on the open sea, even in a heavy swell.

In the first months of the year the campaign against the U-boats did not produce satisfactory results, mainly because the 250lb and 500lb bombs were ineffective and the squadrons did not yet have any depth charges. On January 30th 1940 a Sunderland took part in the pursuit of U55, which had been hit by gunfire from ships. As the U-boat was being harassed by the flying boat, the captain chose to scuttle his vessel. It was not until July 17th 1940 that the next victory over a U-boat would be recorded, attributable to a Sunderland of the Royal Australian Air Force belonging to 10 Squadron.

Because of its great bulk, the Sunderland seemed an easy target for the aircraft of the Luftwaffe. The first engagement occurred on April 3rd 1940 in the North Sea, when six Junkers Ju 88s attacked the Sunderland of Flight Lieutenant Frank Phillips, which was protecting a convoy. The cannon on the German planes had a longer range than the British weapons, which were only accurate at less than 500 yards. The rear gunner in the tail showed remarkable coolness in letting the first attacker approach to within 100 yards before placing the bullets from his four gun barrels right in the nose of the Ju 88, which went down into the sea. A second assailant ended up trailing a plume of black smoke. The rest of the German aircraft preferred to beat a retreat. The same aircrew repeated their exploit on June 21st, just after finding the cruiser *Scharnhorst*. Of the four Messerschmitt Bf 109Es which launched an attack, one was shot down into the sea and the others fled, having all suffered damage to a greater or lesser extent. Flying low over the sea, the flying boat's defences did not leave any blind spots.

The Sunderland also made its contribution to the Norwegian campaign. It spotted the German fleet on the eve of the invasion, and carried the officers responsible for the defence of Narvik. Two months later, on the eve of the French capitulation, a machine from 10 Squadron carried Mountbatten's emissaries to Rabat to win over North Africa to the Free French cause.

From June 1940 the Sunderlands operated in the Mediterranean. One machine made a reconnaissance of Taranto just before the Royal Navy launched its aircraft on a raid on the Italian fleet in November 1940. Four months later, they were also patrolling the South Atlantic, operating from Freetown.

A total of 90 Sunderland Mk 1s were used by eight squadrons. Gradually they were all fitted with radio aerials on the top of the fuselage, which was the visible part of the ASV radar

for detecting targets at sea. Faced with the terrible losses suffered by the convoys, the fight against the U-boats became a priority. Even so the Sunderlands completed other spectacular missions such as that carried out by aircraft of 228 and 230 Squadrons, which at night evacuated first the King of Yugoslavia and his family, then the King of Greece. One of these machines had taken 87 passengers on board, when water began to seep into the interior of the aircraft through the portholes of the lower deck, which were below the water line. The Sunderlands returned to Crete in May to evacuate the British commanding officers caught in the trap of 'Operation Merkur'.

At the end of the year a new version of the aircraft appeared. A turret on top of the fuselage and more powerful armament (the rate of fire of the guns in the rear turret was doubled) were the main improvements, together with the Pegasus XVIII engines fitted with two-stage superchargers giving an output of 1,065hp. The aerials for the Mk 2 ASV radar adorned the rump of the flying boat, of which 43 were made.

To start with, the Mk 2 ASV radar made it possible to detect U-boats which had come to the surface to recharge their batteries during the night and to attack them with depth charges. The

The rear turret of the Sunderland Mk 1 was equipped with four 0.30in machine guns. Although this aircraft's number has been erased by the censors, it is recognizable as belonging to 204 Squadron.

The Sunderland Mk 3 EJ-164 in the new white livery worn by this version, which had improvements to the hull, engines and electrical equipment.

Germans soon came up with a countermeasure against this tactic, which was successfully used in the Bay of Biscay in the summer of 1942. They used Blohm und Voss BV 138Cs, which alighted on the water and waited for the convoys of ships bringing supplies for Great Britain to arrive. They then radioed their position before taking off to take part in the attack and provide cover for the U-boats.

On December 15th 1941, a third version of the Sunderland, with a redesigned main step in the hull to give improved aerodynamics, made its maiden flight. Otherwise the machine was identical to the Mk 2. Of these Sunderland 3s 386 were made; they were slightly heavier and therefore slightly slower than the original version.

As a result of earlier accidents, alighting on the open sea was forbidden. However, on May 28th 1943 a pilot met his death when trying to pick up the six survivors from a bomber. The 10 other members of the crew succeeded in escaping from the flying boat, and were spotted the next day by a pilot from 461 Squadron, Gordon Singleton, who touched down in a sea with troughs 8 feet deep. The 16 survivors were able to get aboard, but there was no possibility of taking off again. A Free French destroyer took the flying boat in tow. One engine was damaged, then the tow broke. Singleton started the remaining three engines, and the machine leapt from wave to wave for three miles before managing to drag itself off the surface. When it was airborne, a hole measuring more than 6ft by 6ft was found in the

bottom of the hull, which made it impossible to touch down on the water. Singleton therefore brought his machine down on a grass landing strip, and did it so brilliantly that the Sunderland was later repaired and able to fly again.

Three days later, another Sunderland returned on two engines after fighting off eight Junkers Ju 88s. In order to counter aerial attacks as well as reply to gunfire from U-boats, the Sunderland was given another four fixed machine guns in the nose operated by the pilot, and others in gun ports, so that in the end it had a total of 18 heavy machine guns.

The considerable numbers produced made it possible to deploy Sunderlands in all the theatres of war, from Iceland to Freetown and from Gibraltar to Ceylon.

To meet the needs of the war in the Pacific, the prototype of the Mk IV was given 1,740hp Bristol Hercules engines. However, the resulting performance was disappointing, and the 10 examples that were built were given the name Seaford for the two prototypes and Solent for the eight production models converted for civil aviation.

The Sunderland V fitted with American 1,200hp Pratt & Whitney Twin Wasp engines was a great success. A first example flew in March 1944, and a second in May. This version could remain airborne for longer – 15 hours instead of 13 – and more particularly it could continue flying fully loaded with two engines out of action on the same side. In addition its radar equipment was much more effective.

The first production examples reached their units in February 1945, and the last of the Sunderland Vs produced at Rochester left the factory on June 14th 1946.

Supplied in sufficient numbers right from the beginning of the war, the Short S.25 Sunderland was in action up to the last day. It was the only flying boat in its class with civil origins, and in spite of the top priority given to the production of fighters and bombers the R.A.F.'s strategists understood the importance of having an open sea patrol aircraft. Certainly its anti-submarine role became more difficult with the advent of craft fitted with schnorkels, which no longer needed to come to the surface to recharge their batteries, but the development of radar detection equipment gave it a chance to find its quarry. Above all the Sunderland demonstrated great flexibility, which enabled it to undertake evacuations in the worst possible conditions as well as air-sea rescue operations.

The Sunderland, having been the only flying boat to take part in the Berlin Air Lift, saw its last action in Korea. The last machines in service with the R.A.F. made their final flight on May 20th 1959. In France the only example still in service flew for the last time on March 24th 1961.

THE SEENOTFLUGBOOTEN

In the course of Germany's rearmament, German strategists had envisaged new roles for the air forces. Seaplanes were not forgotten. During World War I they had occasionally carried out rescue operations when pilots had come down in the sea. In 1939 the Kriegsmarine set up its first Seenotgruppe (sea rescue group) made up of two flights equipped with Heinkel He 59C-2s and He 59D-1s. The latter had six inflatable dinghies and medical equipment for administering first aid; they were registered as civil machines and bore large red crosses. They were to be seen in action in the North Sea and the English Channel during the Battle of Britain. Suspected by the Allies of taking spies to the British Isles, of directing the Stukas or carrying mines, they soon came to be regarded as legitimate targets by the British fighters. Although replaced by the Dornier Do 18-N1 then by the Do 24N-1, the He 59C-2 and D-1 were still operating in 1943.

Increasing specialization

The first seaplane designed to fly with a diesel engine, the Dornier Do 18 took off for the first time on March 15th 1935. The following year production of the military version began. Dornier delivered 39 Dornier Do 18Ds, and Weserflug built 40 of them under licence, followed by 62 Do 18Gs. The production run was completed with 22 Do 18Hs with dual controls. The performance of these aircraft left much to be desired, especially their speed, which was not more than 160mph.

For rescue missions at sea, the Do 18s were modified so that the survivors could enter via the sponsons, gaining access to the interior through a hatch, and by doing away with one fuel tank the passengers had either three seats or two stretchers at their disposal.

During the summer of 1940, five rescue units were set up,

three of them in France (at Cherbourg, Boulogne and Brest) and two in Germany (Norderney and Sylt). From 1941 the Luftwaffe took over control of missions of this kind, and set up in its turn seven sectors for sea searches: two in France, one in Belgium, one in Holland, two in Germany and one in Greece.

If the Do 18 did not leave a lasting impression, this was not the case with its successor, the Dornier Do 24, which the Germans originally had not wanted. The early history of this machine, which was to become a classic of marine aviation, was interesting. The Dutch asked the manufacturer for a machine to replace the Dornier Wal. Claudius Dornier suggested the two-engined Do 18, but this did not satisfy the Dutch requirements, notably the ability to operate over the open sea. The company then put the finishing touches to the Do 24, of which 60 were made in response to a succession of orders from the Dutch. The prototype flew on July 3rd 1937, and the second production example showed exceptional seaworthiness in the course of some highly spectacular trials in the North Sea. 37 Do 24Ks were made and delivered to the Dutch East Indies. After Pearl Harbor, on December 7th 1941, the Dorniers found themselves involved in the fighting against the Japanese, undertaking reconnaissance, bombing and rescue missions and responding to attacks launched by the Kawanishi H6K4 flying boats.

The Japanese offensive swept all before it to such effect that only five Do 24Ks reached Australia at the beginning of March 1942. Taken over by the Royal Australian Air Force (R.A.A.F.), one was assigned to the Dutch special services, which used it for 18 months to carry their agents. The four others were used until December 1944 for training R.A.A.F. pilots.

The Do 24Ks had been fitted with American 1,000hp Wright Cyclone engines. When the Germans started to take an interest in the aircraft, they fitted it with BMW-Bramo 323R-2s of the same power. Designated the Do 24T, this new version could reach 186mph and had a range of up to 2,900 miles. It was also supplied with six stretchers, first aid equipment and two hatches for entering the hull from a boat. Since the building of the

The Dornier Do 18D had insufficient armament and its Jumo diesel engines only produced 600hp.

The end of a Dornier Do 18D shot down by an R.A.F. maritime reconnaissance aircraft off the Norwegian coast.

machine was not considered a priority, it was made under licence by Aviolanda in Holland (170 units) and by CAMS of Sartrouville in France, who made 22 of them in two years. This lower rate of production was the result of industrial sabotage.

In 1941 the Seenotdienst (sea rescue service) was given seven operational bases. In the Mediterranean the Do 24

Tests of the Dornier Do 24V-4 in the open sea enabled the Dutch to confirm the exceptional seaworthiness of the aircraft, of which they ordered 60 examples.

distinguished itself on May 22nd 1941 by picking up 65 survivors from the cruiser *H.M.S. Gloucester*, which had sunk off Crete. In the course of the terrible campaign against Malta, about a thousand sea rescue missions were undertaken, with heavy losses. For example out of the five Do 24Ts that came to the aid of the sailors of the *Roma*, four were shot down and only one returned, with 19 survivors.

The versatility of this trimotor aircraft meant that it could be deployed in the Black Sea to provide cover for the convoys between Odessa and Sebastopol, where 18 Do 24Ts were also to transport 1,000 tons of freight in the month of March 1944. The last Do 24T run during the evacuation of the Crimea was made by a machine with only two engines in working order, and with 40 people on board.

The DO 24T distinguished itself on all fronts, sometimes accomplishing missions that were thought impossible. For instance in June 1942 a Do 24T touched down on a very rough sea, close to a stricken He 115. The waves were breaking against the rear of the flying boat. The crew closed the watertight bulkheads in the hull, picked up the pilots of the Heinkel and set off hydroplaning towards its base, which it reached 24 hours later. Every kind of mission was carried out, including rescue at night. However, from 1943 sea rescue and the evacuation of personnel no longer interested the top brass of the Reich, and in November 1944 production of flying boats was stopped.

The Do 24 continued its career after the war. It was used in France, in Sweden and especially in Spain for air-sea rescue. On August 28th 1971 the last Do 24T-3 ended its career by touching down for the last time on Lake Constance. On this occasion the Dornier company stated that in 30 years of service Do 24s had rescued 11,560 victims of shipwreck. This figure alone justifies the concept of the flying boat as rescuer.

At the beginning of the Second World War, catapult-launched seaplanes were carried on all large warships.

Two Ro.43s are here stowed on board an Italian battleship of the Littorio class.

SHIPBOARD SEAPLANES IN EUROPE

The seaplanes carried on board warships were mainly used as spotters. Distributed among the most important ships, they no longer had any communication problems due to advances in radio technology.

The Heinkel He 114C-1, which, up to 1940, watched over the Soviet convoys in the Baltic and the Black Sea operating from coastal bases, was replaced by the Arado Ar 196, the prototype of which had first flown in 1937. A high-performance two-seater monoplane by virtue of its 960hp BMW 132K engine, the Arado Ar 196A was deployed on the battleship *Graf Spee* and helped it to sink two British cargo ships.

The Arados were carried on board all the German Navy's large vessels, including the battleship *Bismarck*. On May 26th one machine attacked the R.A.F. Catalina which was busy spotting the fleet's movements, but could not prevent it from radioing its position. The battleship was sunk the next day.

Very easy to handle and armed with two 20mm cannons, one machine gun amidships and two at the rear, the Arado was in service right up to the end of the war. It was the most

numerous German seaplane, with 541 machines built including the prototypes.

The British mainly used the Walrus, which was carried both on battleships and on cruisers. Supermarine and Saunders-Roe built 744 of them. The versatility of the Walrus was demonstrated in Somalia in November 1940 when, having bombed troops, the aircraft from *H.M.S. Dorsetshire* guided the bombardment of the port of Dante. In February 1941 a Walrus acted as spotter for the gunfire of ships shelling the port of Genoa. Walruses from coastal bases also undertook numerous air sea rescue missions. From November 1944 onwards, this biplane was gradually replaced by the Supermarine Sea Otter.

In Italy, the standard shipboard seaplane was the I.M.A.M. Ro.43, a two-seater biplane with a central float, with a single-seater version, the Ro.44. The Ro.43 was used for reconnaissance, while the Ro.44 was described as a fighter, although its top speed of just under 200mph made it an easy target. These machines, three of which were assigned to each Italian battleship, were already outdated in 1940. Even so they remained in service until the armistice in September 1943.

Seen being hoisted on board, a catapult-launched I.M.A.M. Ro.43 two-seater reconnaissance aircraft, 42 of which were operational with naval units when Italy entered the war.

Blohm und Voss BV 138C1 in flight over the Black Sea.
This aircraft was often used to give cover to the convoys supplying the troops fighting in the Crimea. In spring 1943 their base was at Constanta in Romania.

THE FLYING SHOE

There had never been any intention of replacing the Do 18 with the Do 24 for long-range reconnaissance, because in 1938 the choice went to the Hamburger Flugzeugbau company with their Ha 138 project, a twin-boom three-engined flying boat with gull-wings. On July 15th 1936, trials showed that the aircraft was a failure. After modifications, in particular conventional wings, the second prototype flew in March 1937. Subsequently the hull was lengthened by 10 feet, and in this new configuration it was given the designation Blohm und Voss BV 138A. Three examples of this flying boat took part in the operations in Norway.

After a short phase in the Atlantic, the BV 138 was principally deployed in the North Sea and the Baltic, the North Atlantic and the Arctic Ocean. Its first operations were notable for victories over a Bristol Blenheim and a Consolidated Catalina, the latter a rare case of a duel between flying boats. The final version, the BV 138C, had two cannons, one in the front turret and one at the rear, and a machine gun in a gun hatch. With its three 865hp Junkers Jumo 205D engines, the BV 138C reached 161mph, had an endurance of 16hrs 30mins and a range of 2,360 miles. Out of a total production of 281 BV 138s, 228 were Cs, 20 were Bs and 25 were As, in addition to six pre-production examples and two prototypes.

In addition to its task of maritime reconnaissance, seeking out and attacking convoys, the BV 138 carried out missions consisting of blowing up acoustic mines, radar reconnaissance and even troop carrying, its fuselage being able to accommodate 10 men. An unusual tactic consisted of alighting on the open sea and waiting, for three days if need be, until a convoy came along. The aircraft took part in numerous engagements, the most famous being that with Convoy PQ-17 connecting Iceland and Murmansk, which ended with the loss of two-thirds of the Allied cargo ships in the course of this combined action.

The use of aircraft carriers to provide protection changed the course of events. In September 1942 on the occasion of their first engagement, Sea Hurricanes from a carrier subjected the strength of the BV 138C to a severe test; it returned to base badly battered after an hour and a half of combat. In the summer of 1943 BV 138Cs operated for three months from a base set up inside Soviet territory by German U-boats.

From 1943 on the aircraft, nicknamed the 'Flying Shoe', suffered heavy losses because of its low speed and the omnipresent Allied fighters. One of the last survivors touched down on one of the Berlin lakes under a hail of fire at midnight on May 1st 1945. Its mission was to take two sealed envelopes, but the pilot, Wolfgang Klemusch, refused to take them because the bearer could not say what they were. Klemuscn then took on board 10 wounded, whom he flew to Copenhagen. It was later discovered that the envelopes contained Adolf Hitler's last will and testament ...

Manoeuvring the 'Flying Shoe' on the ground was facilitated by the use of a special trolley. The front turret housed a 20mm cannon.

The BV 138C1 could be catapult-launched with an all-up weight of 40,000lb. An aircraft with its engines at full throttle waits to take off from the *Westfalen*.

THE WAR IN THE PACIFIC

On December 7th 1941, the surprise attack on Pearl Harbor marked the beginning of the war in the Pacific. The huge expanse of sea where the Japanese confronted the Americans and their allies was an area particularly favourable to the development of the naval air arm in general and the seaplane in particular. Never in history was such a large number of seaplanes thrown into battle, but their role was primarily confined to reconnaissance, surveillance and transport, their engagements limited to attacks on ships and submarines.

In spite of remarkable design work by Japanese engineers, there was never a fighter or bomber seaplane that could match its landplane counterparts. On the American side, the reliability of engines became such that covering huge distances across the ocean no longer demanded the extra security of a boat hull, except for patrol aircraft operating over the open sea. The

development of aircraft carriers relegated the seaplane to certain specific tasks, but this did not prevent the American aircraft industry from producing more of them than all the other combatants put together.

The Americans were also more judicious in their choices. Between 1936 and 1945, the Japanese only made 433 flying boats to cover bombing, reconnaissance and transport requirements, while the Americans produced 3,120 patrol aircraft and 270 cargo planes. The Japanese gave priority to reconnaissance or spotting close to carrier ships or bases, building 3,460 seaplanes of this category as against the U.S.A.'s 3,140. Convinced that there was no point in the exercise, the Americans contented themselves with experimentally fitting floats to the Grumman F4F-3S Wildcat, a shipboard fighter – which confirmed the reduction in performance caused by doing this – whereas their enemies built 424 Nakajima A6M2-Ns and Kawanishi N1K1 Kyofus.

Symbolizing American power in the Pacific, Catalinas fly over the impressive armada which is preparing to recapture Luzon in the Philippines in January 1945.

After a twenty-minute chase through the clouds, a Kawanishi H6K5 has just caught a burst of fire from a Consolidated PBY-4.
The wing is beginning to burn. This incident took place off the Truk Islands.

The classic flying boat, a PBY-6A, flies above the waters of the Pacific.

235 examples of the last version of the Catalina were made in the final stages of the war.

THE CATALINA

When Isaac Machlin Laddon started his studies for the Consolidated Model 28 at the beginning of 1933, he was only thinking of improving the P2Y-1 Ranger, of which 23 had been built. He never suspected that what he was designing was the prototype for the most successful aircraft in the history of marine aviation, the Catalina, of which more than 3,400 would be built in the United States, Canada and the Soviet Union.

The PBY-2 entered service with the U.S. Navy in May 1937.

Of the 60 PBY-2s made, 46 were still operational in December 1941.

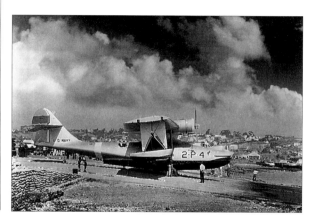

Designated the XP3Y-1, the prototype flew for the first time on March 21st 1935. A flying boat with two engines (825hp Pratt & Whitney Twin Wasp), it had a parasol wing with floats that retracted to form the wing tips. The wings could carry up to a ton of bombs, which made these flying boats bombers as well as patrol aircraft. The series designation was PBY-1, in which the Y indicated that it was built by Consolidated. Sixty PBY-1s were delivered to the U.S. Navy from October 1936, then 50 PBY-2s, 66 PBY-3s and 32 PBY-4s, each new version being given more powerful engines. Richard Archbold bought two PBYs, which he called Guba I and II. The Russians bought Guba I and a licence to build about 150 units at Taganrog with the designation GST. Guba II made the first flight round the world by a seaplane over the great circle route.

With the outbreak of war in Europe, the U.S. Navy was given the task of carrying out 'neutrality patrols' and placed a record order for 200 PBY-5s equipped with 1,050hp Twin Wasp engines. An amphibian version appeared with the designation PBY-5A. The R.A.F. also acquired some PBY-5s, which were given the name 'Catalina'. It was a Catalina II which spotted the *Bismarck* on May 26th 1941. Australia and Canada also bought

Catalinas, the aircraft's name having meanwhile been made official by the U.S. Navy.

On December 7th 1941, at 6.33am, a PBY-5 of sea patrol squadron VP-14 piloted by Ensigns Tanner and Greevy detected an unidentified submarine a mile or more off the entrance to Pearl Harbor. At 7.57am a hail of bombs came down on the harbour installations. After the first wave of Japanese aircraft had passed, the few undamaged aircraft were given the order to locate the Japanese fleet, but just as they were trying to clear a path through the piles of debris the second attacking wave was unleashed on the harbour. Altogether 92 U.S. Navy seaplanes, mostly PBYs, were destroyed and 31 damaged.

The first PBY-5 engaged in combat was returning from a mission at the time of the attack on Pearl Harbor. Its pilot, Ensign F. Meyer, spotting a formation of Japanese aircraft, flew his machine low over the water so that the enemy fighters could not approach from below, in his guns' blind spot. This tactic enabled him to resist attack, and even to hit an enemy aircraft. But he failed in his mission to locate the Japanese fleet.

At the same time the Philippines became the scene of a similar operation which preceded the invasion of the islands. The PBY-4s of VP-101 and VP-102 suffered considerable losses: 10 aircraft out of 24 in four days. Six Catalinas were sent on a mission to bomb Jolo on December 27th, after a flight of 870 miles. Two returned to base.

The surviving seaplanes were regrouped at Surabaja in Indonesia, and at Darwin in Australia. Out of 45 Catalinas used by patrol squadron Patwing 10, only 12 were operational by the beginning of February. The attack on Darwin on February 19th 1942 destroyed three of these. On April 29th two Catalinas evacuated 50 officers and nurses from Corregidor, accomplishing the longest rescue mission ever attempted.

The Japanese offensive seemed irresistible. A major battle

was brewing for the control of Midway, a small archipelago developed by Pan American. On June 3rd 1942 Ensign Jack Reid discovered Admiral Yamamoto's invasion fleet, so what had not come off at Pearl Harbor was achieved here by a PBY-5A. The armada was located 750 miles from its objective. On June 4th at 5.20am the Japanese combat squadrons were spotted, and at 7am the battle of the aircraft carriers began.

The Catalinas were used to search for survivors. Twenty-seven Americans were picked up, among them Ensign George Gay, the only remaining member of VT-8, who was rescued after 30 hours in the water.

The Battle of Midway is now presented as a great American victory, but at the time this was not so obvious, all the more so as the diversion carried out by the Japanese in the Aleutians seemed to be going in their favour.

The weather conditions prevailing on this string of islands, which extend from Alaska's western tip, were so terrible that pilots feared them more than enemy aircraft. With 100mph winds, freezing rain and impenetrable fogs, not to mention almost polar temperatures, there were many difficulties and dangers. At dawn on June 3rd, a Catalina located the Japanese after the attack on Dutch Harbor. A PBY-5 made a bid to torpedo the aircraft carrier *Junyo*, but one engine was hit by gunfire and the flying boat dropped its charges into the sea and vanished

Like many other American aircraft, the PBY got the name it was to be known by in the R.A.F.
This machine is the very first assessed by the British, hence the first true Catalina.

A Coastal Command Catalina operating from Ulster moored to a buoy.
The crew member seems to be experiencing some difficulty.

This is one of the Catalinas which took part in the hunt for the *Bismarck*.
Note the excellent visibility provided by the side blisters in the rear of the fuselage.

In the Aleutians, the PBY-5As took part in all the action in dreadful conditions.
A Catalina amphibian is taking off from a makeshift runway, throwing mud and snow in all directions.

into a cloud, returning to base on one engine.

The Japanese came ashore on two islands at the western end of the archipelago. Operating from the aircraft carrier *U.S.S. Gillis*, the Catalinas mounted an unrelenting attack on the enemy positions for more than a day, until the stock of bombs on the ship was exhausted. The flying boats dive-bombed their targets for greater accuracy, pulling out at 500 feet and nearly touching the waves before using their speed to gain altitude and disappear in the clouds. The intensive bombing raids lasted for four days. The PBY-5s destroyed numerous installations on the ground, hit several ships and sank three Kawanishi H6K flying boats at their moorings.

Once the bombing campaign was over, the Catalinas returned to their more usual tasks: anti-submarine warfare, rescue missions and sea patrols. In the course of one reconnaissance mission a Catalina discovered a Mitsubishi A6M2 Zero which had landed in a field on the island of Unalaska. The damaged machine was recovered by the Americans, who repaired it and studied it, then flew it against their fighters. This enabled them to perfect tactics to counter the Zero, which up to then had been considered invincible.

The war effort resulted in remarkable production figures for the Catalina in the USA: 640 PBY-5s between 1940 and 1944, 802 PBY-5As between 1941 and 1945 and 176 PBY-6s in 1945.

The reconquest of the islands gave the Catalinas plenty of opportunities to show what they could do. At Guadalcanal General Geiger's personal aircraft torpedoed a supply ship. During this long battle, which started in August 1942 and was to last for six months, the Catalina crews perfected the 'Black Cat' strategy: black-painted Catalinas flew at night, loaded with bombs and torpedoes which they used whenever they located a

suitable target. In the Battle of the Solomon Islands, PBY-5s equipped with radar caused havoc among the supply convoys for the Japanese troops, called the 'Tokyo Express'. Their ability to take so much punishment from flak bordered on the miraculous.

Catalinas also brought supplies to the Australian observers who kept watch on enemy shipping movements, and picked them up when required, but it was on their rescue missions that these aircraft covered themselves with glory. For example, on February 15th 1944 Lieutenant Nathan G. Gordon recovered 25 airmen in three touchdowns during the same mission, each time under fire from nearby enemy guns, an exploit which won him the Medal of Honor, the highest American decoration. The record number for a rescue is attributed to Lieutenant Joe F. Ball, whose Air Force Catalina took off on December 4th 1944 with 56 survivors from the destroyer *U.S.S. Cooper*.

PBY-5s and 5As also took part in the fight against the U-boat in the Atlantic and the Mediterranean, operated by the U.S. Navy and the British, Australian, New Zealand, South African, Free French, Norwegian and Dutch East Indies forces. To satisfy demand, 350 rolled off assembly lines other than those at San Diego in the United States, while 731 were produced in Canada under the name Canso, mainly for the Commonwealth countries. Taking into account the 150 GSTs made by the Russians, the total production comes to the record figure of 3,431 aircraft.

Although already technically outdated at the beginning of the war, the Catalina owed its success to its reliability under any conditions, to its versatility and to its extraordinary ability to absorb punishment from enemy fire. After the war, 23 countries used the Catalina for rescue and patrol missions at sea. Some machines were used for civilian duties, the best known being the PBY-6A of Yves Cousteau, at the controls of which his son met his death on the Tagus in July 1979.

A PBY-6A leaving the factory in New Orleans.
Note the nose turret equipped with two 0.50in machine guns and the radar mounted on top of the cockpit.

The seagoing capabilities of the Catalina are not being put to the test on this calm sea.
The floats retract into the ends of the wings in flight, forming the wing tips.

The Kawanishi H6K5 Mavis was the final version of the staple Japanese patrol flying boat.
This four-engined aircraft had a better performance than the American Catalina and Coronado.

THE KAWANISHI H6K MAVIS

The Kawanishi H6K Mavis was the Japanese equivalent of the Catalina. A four-engined aircraft with a parasol wing fitted with 840hp Nakajima Hikari engines, the first prototype flew on July 14th 1936. Although under-engined, the H6K1 showed that it had excellent handling on the water and could undertake long-range maritime reconnaissance, as well as torpedoing ships and bombing. Three other prototypes preceded the first production version, the H6K2 equipped with 1,000hp Mitsubishi Kinsei 43 engines. Ten examples were produced in 1938, while two H6K3 transports were delivered the following year, as well as 18 H6K4s, the first of the series production version, of which 129 were made up to 1942.

Four H6K2s were used to apply pressure on the Soviet authorities at the time of the negotiations on fishing agreements

On May 10th 1945, a Mavis was shot down by a Coronado in one of the last duels between flying boats.

in the Sea of Okhotsk in January 1939. Six examples were subsequently deployed in the Marshall Islands in order to develop strategies for use in open sea, and to photograph the sites which would become objectives. When Japan went to war, the Imperial Navy had 66 H6Ks divided among four Kokutai (squadrons). The first bombing mission was carried out on December 9th 1941. Six aircraft attacked the Dutch seaplane tender *Heron* on December 31st, and five days later began the raids on Rabaul. H6Ks went on night bombing missions while also undertaking marine reconnaissance enabling them to locate the carrier *U.S.S. Lexington,* which was unable to come to the aid of Rabaul.

While the H6K excelled in its role of a marine patrol aircraft with a range of 3,400 miles and an endurance of 27 hours, the machine suffered from a lack of protective armour and self-sealing tanks, which made it very vulnerable to gunfire. The last version, the H6K5, of which 36 were made in 1942, was given 1,300hp Kinsei engines and improved armament, but its weaknesses were not eliminated.

H6Ks were used throughout the war, bombing the Australian coast in July 1942, but always in numbers that were too small in all the theatres of war. It was increasingly relegated to the role of a transport aircraft, its combat function having passed to its successor, the Kawanishi H8K. Thirty-six Mavises were in fact built as transports, the total number of H6Ks amounting to 215, or one fifteenth of the production of Catalinas. The technical superiority of the Japanese aircraft never made up for its inferiority in numbers.

JAPANESE FIGHTER SEAPLANES

Of all the participants in the war, the Japanese were the only nation to build fighter seaplanes, initially by mounting a Mitsubishi A6M2 Zero on floats – a job performed by Nakajima – then by designing the Kawanishi N1K Kyofu, which, deprived of its floats, was to become one of the best fighters of the Second World War: the N1K1-J George.

In February 1941 Nakajima started on the design for a seaplane with the task of providing air cover for troops during disembarkation. Fitted with a large central float which also served as a fuel tank, the A6M2-N made its first flight on December 7th 1941, and the first production example left the works on in April 1942. Called 'Rufe' by the Americans, this aircraft was deployed at Guadalcanal and then in the Aleutians, where the absence of airfields made its use essential. However, instead of being given an attacking role, it was soon put on defensive missions. Its maximum speed of 267mph at 16,000 feet was inadequate when confronted by American land-based fighters; only its manoeuvrability enabled it to escape hostile fire. It was rapidly relegated to training units, and the surviving examples vainly tried to resist the devastating raids of the Boeing B-29s in 1945. Nakajima built a total of 327 A6M2-Ns up to September 1943.

From September 1940, Kawanishi was working on the design of a fighter seaplane with a large central float. The first N1K1 flew on May 6th 1942. The contra-rotating propellers caused too many problems and were replaced by a conventional three-bladed propeller which produced a very marked torque effect on takeoff.

The Kyofu which came off the production lines in 1943 had very good performance figures, notably a maximum speed of 285mph, but it was its flying qualities that were particularly remarkable. The Imperial Navy wanted to replace its A6M2-Ns with the N1K1, but only 97 were built before giving way to its

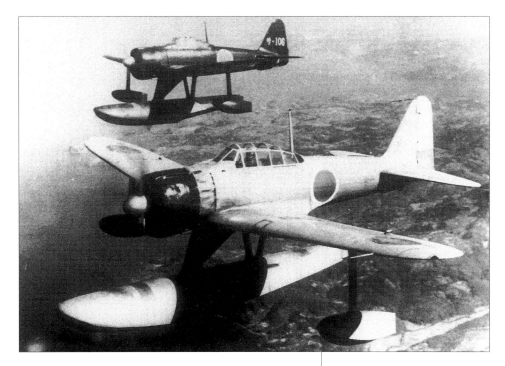

landplane version, the N1K1-J Shiden, of which 1,000 were made. In spite of its qualities, the Kyofu played an ancillary role in the fighting; in Borneo it joined the A6M2-Ns as part of the Otsu Kokutai based on Lake Biwa. Japanese engineers had undoubtedly designed the best fighter seaplane one could hope for, but the concept itself embodied limitations which prevented it from becoming a viable combat aircraft.

JAPANESE RECONNAISSANCE SEAPLANES

For reconnaissance and spotter duties, the Japanese produced 3,460 aircraft as opposed to 3,140 in the case of their American adversaries, although the latter were fighting on two fronts. No less than six different designs come into this category of aircraft.

The Kawanishi E7K1 was a three-seater biplane with a 620hp Hiro engine. It had three machine guns, could mount four 60lb bombs, and flew for the first time on February 6th 1933. A second more powerful version, designated E7K2, saw the light of day in November 1938. It remained in first-line service until 1943, providing protection for convoys and anti-submarine patrols, as well as reconnaissance. Called 'Alfs' by the Americans, 530 examples of the E7K1 and E7K2 were built.

The Mitsubishi F1M2 was the sole seaplane in the reconnaissance category to go into series production. Four F1M1 prototypes showed that the biplane porpoised on takeoff and had unsatisfactory flying qualities. The F1M2 eliminated these faults so successfully that 1,114 left the production line. The

The Nakajima A6M2-N Rufe was the first Japanese attempt to produce a fighter seaplane. It was in fact a Mitsubishi A6M2 Zero fitted with floats.

The Kawanishi N1K1 Rex had little success, unlike its landplane equivalent of which 1,435 were made under the name Shiden.

The Aichi E13A1 was the Japanese reconnaissance seaplane most used in the war in the Pacific.
It could remain airborne for nearly 15 hours, which made it an excellent convoy escort.

The Kawanishi E15K1 Shiun was a reconnaissance aircraft that was let down by its mechanical complexity (due to the contra-rotating propellers) and its removable central float, which made it difficult to control.

aircraft, given the American code name Pete, served on all fronts and added to its intended role pursuit and the support of disembarkation operations. Fitted with 820hp Nakajima engines, the F1M2 could reach a speed of 230mph.

The Yokosuka E14Y1 had the unique claim to fame that it was the only Japanese aircraft to bomb mainland American soil when, in September 1942, Lieutenant Fujita dropped four 150lb bombs on the forests of Oregon, having taken off from the submarine I-25. First produced in 1939, the Glen, as it was known, was a two-seater monoplane able to fly at 150mph. It was carried in a special caisson on the submarine. E14Y1s, of which 126 were made, undertook reconnaissance missions to Pearl Harbor, and then flew in all sectors of operation from the Aleutians to Madagascar.

Designed in 1939, the Kawanishi E15K1 was a high-performance reconnaissance seaplane, fitted with contra-rotating propellers and a removable central float, which could fly at 292mph at an altitude of 20,000 feet. In 1943 six E15K1s based on the cruiser *Oyodo* were sent to the Palau Islands to be assessed for a combat role, but their single 7.7mm machine gun and poor armour made them easy targets for the American fighters, all the more so as the mechanism for releasing the central float did not function correctly. A total of only 15 E15K1s were built.

The Aichi E13A1 had a production run of 1,418, which gave it a very important place in the Japanese arsenal. The prototype flew in 1938, and production examples went into service in 1941 on cruisers and aircraft carriers. Given the American code name Jake, the E13A1 could fly at 230mph, had a range of 1,250 miles and an endurance of 15 hours. They were used as bombers when enemy defences were relatively weak, as torpedo aircraft, as transports for V.I.P.s, as rescue seaplanes and, at the end of conflict, as kamikazes; to these numerous missions were added open-sea patrols.

The Aichi E16A Zuiun was the worthy successor of the E13A1. Made entirely of metal, this two-seater had two 20mm cannons in the wings and a machine gun firing backwards, a considerable improvement over the Jake. Moreover it could dive-bomb with a 500lb bomb. 256 examples were built. Known as the Paul, it could fly at 273mph thanks to its 1,560hp Mitsubishi engine. The Zuiuns suffered heavy losses in the Philippines in 1944, and were among the waves of kamikazes which attacked the American fleet off Okinawa in 1945.

AMERICAN RECONNAISSANCE SEAPLANES

Like the other navies, the U.S. Navy carried floatplanes on all its larger ships. Originally intended for surveillance close to the fleet and for directing gunfire, they were soon used for other purposes, both for picking up crew members lost at sea and for ferrying officers.

The Curtiss SOC Seagull was a biplane whose prototype flew on June 19th 1933. The SOC-1 was designed to start with as an amphibian with a central float and two removable side floats, allowing a conventional undercarriage to be fitted. Made in three versions up to 1938, the Seagull was supplied to all the shipboard reconnaissance flights. The following year the SOC-3 reached 161mph, but this poor performance did not prevent it from taking part in the great battles of the Pacific war, from Guadalcanal to the Gilbert Islands.

In 1944 the survivors of the 262 examples made were overhauled to continue in service instead of the Curtiss SO3C, their intended replacement, which had turned out to be a disaster in operation.

The Grumman J2F Duck was a descendant of the Loenings. Its main task was light transport (it took two passengers), but it was also used for photography, making smoke screens, towing targets, evacuating the wounded, and particularly for air sea rescue. Between 1936 and 1945, 525 Ducks were produced. This biplane had a maximum speed of 168mph and completed numerous missions at sea, rescuing crews for the U.S. Navy and the Marine Corps.

The Chance Vought OS2U Kingfisher, of which 1,519 were made, made its maiden flight on July 20th 1938. It was a two-seater monoplane which could be converted into a landplane. A total of 536 of them were in service in December 1941, which made it the most used seaplane at that time. The final version, the OS2U-3, of which 1,306 were built in 1941-42, could reach 165mph and had a range of 800 miles.

Kingfishers were attached to land-based patrol squadrons, responsible for locating German U-boats in the Caribbean. In the Pacific they accomplished innumerable rescue missions, most famously, on November 12th 1942, picking up the ace of air aces, Eddie Rickenbacker, who had been the victim of an accident three weeks earlier.

Although 801 Curtiss SO3C Seamews were made, the aircraft turned out to be an unfortunate failure. The prototype flew on October 6th 1939. Intended to replace the SOC as soon as possible, the first SO3C-1 did not become operational until July 15th 1942, but in addition to its deplorable flying characteristics its performance was worse than the SOC Seagull's. It was therefore relegated to training tasks, while a certain number were fitted with undercarriages and converted into radio-controlled aircraft.

The Curtiss SC-1 Seahawk represents the culmination of the single-float shipboard seaplane. The prototype made its first flight on February 16th 1943, and the production version arrived on the *U.S.S. Guam* in October 1944. Its maximum speed of 307mph made the SC-1 the fastest of the reconnaissance seaplanes. It became operational in Borneo in June 1945. Before the final victory over Japan, the production lines at Columbus turned out 560 Seahawks.

The Vought OS2U-3 Kingfisher was the U.S. Navy's standard shipboard seaplane.
It showed remarkable versatility, and more than one pilot who had been shot down owed his life to it; it would come along after the Catalinas in air-sea battles.

The Curtiss SC-1 Seahawk was greatly superior to the other American catapult-launched seaplanes, but the fact that it was a single-seater effectively ruled it out for rescue missions.

The Martin PBM-1 Mariner was originally built with retractable floats, while the PBM-3 and subsequent versions had fixed floats.

THE MARINER

In the spring of 1937, the Martin company received a contract on the basis of their design for the XPBM-1, a twin-engined patrol flying boat intended to replace the Catalina. The prototype flew on February 18th 1939, its characteristic features being a gull wing and a very deep hull. Tests led to an important modification of the tailplane. Twenty production PBM-1s arrived with their squadron in September 1940. The main series of the Mariner was the PBM-3, of which 677 examples were made. About 50 aircraft were used as transports to supply anti-submarine bases set up from the Caribbean to Brazil; theses PBM-3Rs arrived in formation in April 1942. The PBM-3Cs, 3Ds and 3Ss were deployed in the Atlantic to play an active part in the battle of the convoys and had advanced radar equipment to locate German U-boats.

On June 30th 1942 a PBM-1 sank the U-boat U-158 off Bermuda; this was the first victim of an American seaplane. Between May and August 1943 Mariners destroyed seven German U-boats. Seventeen Mariner squadrons patrolled in the Atlantic as against only one in the Pacific, but at the end of the year 11 squadrons were deployed at a floating seaplane base off Saipan in order to protect the Mariana Islands invasion forces. In

spite of a maximum speed of only 211mph, the aircraft was liked by its aircrews for its comfort and for its armament, which comprised eight 0.50in machine guns and 7,000lb of bombs. In addition to patrols, both day and night, the Mariner carried out rescue missions and transport of the wounded.

The PBM-3 did not have enough power to fly satisfactorily on one engine, but the PBM-5 which followed it on the production lines in September 1944 used 2,100hp Pratt & Whitney R2800-22 engines. This aircraft's cruising speed was only 145mph but it had a range of 2,500 miles with a 3,500lb bomb load. It took part in the reconquest of the Philippines, then in the capture of Okinawa. This Martin flying boat was the only combat aircraft whose production run began before the war and continued after the armistice. Altogether 1,366 aircraft were built.

However, the Mariner was not as successful as the Catalina in other countries. The R.A.F. preferred the later Sunderland versions, but the Australians used them, and the U.S. Navy passed on surplus machines to Holland, Argentina and Uruguay, and to the U.S. Coast Guard. The PBM-5As were among the first aircraft to see action in Korea. In the mid-fifties they were withdrawn in favour of the Martin Marlin, and the Coast Guard took them off their patrols in 1958.

THE FINEST OF ITS DAY

On August 28th 1938, Kawanishi received the order for a patrol flying boat which was to replace the H6K. The company took up the challenge. The H8K was designed to have a maximum speed of 276mph, cruising at 183mph, with a range of 4,600 miles, as compared with 239mph, 161mph and 3,400 miles respectively of the H6K. Defensive armament increased from one to five 20mm cannons as well as four machine guns. The H8K could also fly on two engines without losing altitude. On December 30th 1940 Lieutenant Hiromitsu Ito took off in the first prototype equipped with four 1,530hp Mitsubishi Kasei II engines. Seaworthiness proved to be so poor at high taxiing speeds that it was necessary to increase the depth of the hull, and modifications were made to prevent the spray from being blown by the propellers onto the pilot's windscreen.

Three pre-production examples were built in 1941, and 13 the following year. Called 'Emily' by the Americans, two H8K1s carried out their first mission on March 3rd 1942. Taking off from Wotje in the Marshall Islands, they touched down in the Frigate Islands archipelago and were refuelled by submarines before going on to drop their bombs near Pearl Harbor, in order to give the impression that a new attack was starting just before the invasion of Midway.

From 1943 onwards, the Emily gradually replaced the Mavis, so 112 H8K-2s left the production line. This definitive version was fitted with 1,850hp Kasei 22 engines which gave a speed of 282mph, a record for this category of flying boat. The protection of the fuel tanks was improved, as was the armament. The aircraft was used equally for bombing, torpedoing, sea patrols and anti-submarine warfare.

The advance of the American forces and their increasing powers of devastation resulted in the destruction of numerous H8K-2s, which none the less remained the most difficult aircraft to destroy in aerial combat. 36 H8K-2L transports were used to carry 25 passengers and 2,500lb of freight over a distance of 2,730 miles. These Emilys were used to evacuate officers of the general staff both by day and by night. In the last days of the war, the few surviving aircraft took on the task of pathfinders for kamikaze raids.

On November 11th 1945 Lieutenant Tsuneo Hitsuji took off from Takume for Yokohama, where the U.S. Navy was to dispatch to the United States the last of the H8K2s still in flying condition, in order to have it evaluated. He was accompanied by Lieutenant Silver, who admitted to him during the flight: "Japan may have lost the war, but the H8K is the best flying boat in the world."

This Kawanishi H8K2 Emily was photographed just before being shot down by an American aircraft.
Technically the H8K2 is considered to have been the best flying boat of its generation.

The Blohm und Voss BV 222V1 made numerous flights in the service of the Afrika Korps in the autumn of 1941, without any armament.

Leaving the factory, BV 222V1 has a civil registration as the aircraft was originally ordered by Deutsche Lufthansa.

The Blohm und Voss BV 238 was the largest and heaviest flying boat transport in the Second World War.

Its career was limited to test flights in the spring of 1944 before it was sunk by Mustangs of the U.S.A.A.F.

THE LEVIATHANS

In the competition between seaplanes and landplanes, the heavyweight flying boats undoubtedly provided much of the interest in the Second World War. The most massive of them all weighed 80 tons, half as much again as a Boeing B-29 Superfortress bomber. However none of the giant flying boats reached the stage of large scale series production: the combatants preferred machines of more modest dimensions, which were still adequate for the transportation of personnel and freight.

The German giants

Before the war Deutsche Lufthansa had already carried out numerous transatlantic mail flights. Their main ambition remained passenger transport, and the programme set up in 1936 culminated in the order for three Blohm und Voss BV 222s designed by Richard Vogt.

The first prototype completed its test flight on September 7th 1940. This six-engined aircraft carried a civil registration, which was soon to be replaced by a military number when it made a series of flights in the service of the Luftwaffe. It showed that it could carry up to 92 passengers, or 72 on stretchers, over short distances, at a maximum speed of 239mph. Altogether 12 BV 222s were used by the Luftwaffe, their primary task being the transport of supplies to the Afrika Korps. Seven of these flying

boats (given the name 'Wiking') carried out this work in such difficult conditions that it resulted in the loss of three of them. Touching down at night, without any marker lights in order not to betray their presence to the British bombers, must have terrified more than one pilot!

In 1942 the third prototype was assessed in the Bay of Biscay for maritime reconnaissance. Its task was to locate convoys and to pass on their positions to the U-boats and bombers. On June 10th 1943 it was sunk at Biscarosse by R.A.F. fighters, at the same time as the fifth prototype. During a night mission in October 1943, a BV 222C shot down an Avro Lancaster.

The six remaining Wiking aircraft went to the Baltic, where they flew out the sick and wounded up to the end of hostilities. The last BV 222C was assessed at Felixstowe before being assigned to 201 Squadron, with which it operated until 1947.

From July 1941, the Blohm und Voss engineers were working on the design of the BV 238, which was to become the largest and heaviest of all the flying boats to have flown during the war. Designed as a long-range transport seaplane, capable of carrying out bombing and maritime reconnaissance missions, the BV 238 was the culmination of studies undertaken in 1940 for a replacement for the BV 138. Numerous changes in the specification resulted in a contract being signed for four prototypes.

The BV 238 did not start its trials until April 1944. It looked like a scaled up BV 222, fitted with six 1,730hp DB 603A engines. Its two-step hull had in fact eight small steps after the first one, and the length-to-beam ratio had a factor of ten, much higher than the usual six or even the eight of the Wiking. Its hydrodynamic and aerodynamic performance benefited from this boldness. The hull opened at the front to allow direct loading of the lower deck. The wing was built around a welded tubular spar containing fuel, while flaps ran along the trailing edge as far as the ailerons, and a passageway made it possible for a mechanic to reach the engines during flight. The flight controls were partly power-assisted, partly manual.

With a wingspan of 197ft 4½ins, a length of 142ft 8½ins and a height of 43ft 11fiins, the BV 238's only rival for sheer size was the Tupolev ANT-20 (PS-124) landplane, whose corre-sponding measurements were 206ft 7½ins, 111ft 10ins and 25ft 3ins. The flying boat weighed 80 tons on takeoff, or twice as much as the Soviet landplane.

According to American archives, BV 238 V1, the only one to have flown, was destroyed at its moorings on September 18th 1944 by Lieutenant Ben Drew. With the second prototype nearly complete and three aircraft under construction, flying boat production was stopped on October 1st 1944 as all the efforts of the German aircraft industry were concentrated on war material for the defence of the homeland. Even so, because of the extraordinary technical challenge that it took up, the BV 238 merits a place in the history of the seaplane.

210 examples of the Consolidated PB2Y-3 were built. The Coronado began its career as a maritime patrol aircraft before being used as a transport.

The American truckers

The Consolidated PB2Y Coronado, which made its first flight on December 17th 1937, was intended to take over from the Catalina as a bomber seaplane. It had a very deep hull, and could carry a bombload of 11,000lb. However, the XPB2Y-1 showed such a marked weaving instability that the tailplane had to be completely redesigned, while the hull became even deeper. The prototype, nicknamed 'Blue Goose', was used from August 1939 to carry the highest-ranking officers in the U.S. Navy.

The first production example flew on November 22nd 1940, but only five PB2Y-2s were delivered. The sixth acted as the prototype for the PB2Y-3, of which 200 examples rolled off the production line at San Diego between June 1942 and October 1943. This version had better armour plating, self-sealing tanks and eight 0.50in machine guns. The additional weight of three tons when empty made the aircraft underpowered, since the 1,200hp Pratt & Whitney R1830-88 engines did not offer any corresponding increase in power.

The U.S. Navy tried out the technique of assisted takeoff with rockets in order to be able to use the Coronado with its fully laden weight of 67,900lb. It took part in the bombing of the Marshall Islands, but was quickly replaced by the PB4Y-1, which was the naval version of the famous Consolidated B-24 Liberator. The Coronado was then used for maritime reconnaissance missions and transport duties. It could carry 44 passengers or 16,000lb of cargo, and played an active part in the evacuation of the wounded from the terrible battle of Iwo Jima. However, since it could not satisfactorily replace the Catalina, the Coronado quickly disappeared from the strength of the U.S. Navy, which by 1946 no longer had any .

The Martin XPB2M-1R Mars occupies second place among the giant flying boats built during the war, but unlike the Blohm und Voss BV 238V1 it did occasionally see service, and six production aircraft were to be produced after the war. Ordered in 1939, the XPB2M-1 was launched in November 1941. On December 5th an engine caught fire, its propeller pierced the hull, and the engine fell into the Middle River. Repairs to the aircraft took a month.

After numerous tests, the prototype took off on June 23rd 1942. Powered by four 2,200hp Wright R3350-18 engines, the aircraft had a wingspan of 200ft, a length of 117ft 3ins and a height of 38ft 4½ins. The dry weight was 75,400lb, increasing to 143,700lb loaded. The tests proved that the Mars could carry a load of up to 30,000lb. In October 1942 on its final test flight it covered 4,600 miles at an average of 143mph.

Its top speed of 220mph combined with its size made it an easy target, and the industrial input that would be needed for series production was so enormous that the U.S. Navy decided to convert the prototype into a transport seaplane with the designation XPB2M-1R. All the armament was removed, as well as the armour plating and the bomb racks. The floor was reinforced and cargo-handling equipment installed. In its new configuration XPB2M-1R touched down at the Patuxent River base in Maryland.

Three days later, the Mars flew 6 tons of cargo to Natal, covering 4,375 miles at an average of 153mph. In January 1944 the flying boat left VR-8, which was used for the training of crews, for VR-2 in California. Up to 1945, it made 78 return flights between San Francisco and Honolulu, carrying 1,360 tons of cargo and personnel, including more than 100 tons of blood for those wounded at Iwo Jima.

The U.S. Navy ordered 20 JRM-1s. The main difference between them and the prototype Mars was the conventional tailplane, which increased the aircraft's height to 47ft 10½ins. The contours of the hull were altered, the engines now provided an output of 2,400hp and interior was completely rearranged.

The first JRM-1 flew in July 1945. On August 5th it crashed into Chesapeake Bay. Four JRM-1s and one JRM-2 were produced after the war and served in VR-2 until August 22nd 1956. The four surviving aircraft then started a new career in Canada in a fire-fighting role. Two aircraft belonging to Forest Industries Flying Tankers were still being used in 1996 to put out forest fires in British Columbia.

A British attempt

In 1940, the R.A.F. issued a specification for long-range reconnaissance flying boats which were intended to replace the Sunderland. When the Short S.35 Shetland made its maiden flight on December 14th 1944, it was assigned to troop transport. With a wingspan of 150ft 4ins, a length of 110ft and a height of 38ft 8ins, the Shetland had to be lightened so that it could take off, because with its original weight of 124,740lb the hull was so deep in the water that the floats broke the surface and braked the aircraft. With its four 2,500hp Bristol Centaurus XI engines, the S.35 had a top speed of 260mph and a range of 4,400 miles.

Test flights had concentrated on improving the flying controls, but the flying boat was burnt at its moorings on January 28th 1946. A second prototype, the Shetland II, made its first flight on September 17th 1947. Initially intended for B.O.A.C., it was scrapped in the early fifties. The civil derivatives of the Sunderland were to survive it by a decade.

CHAPTER 5

The Decline

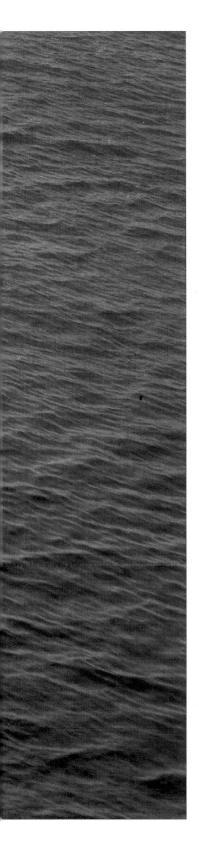

AFTER THE WAR, BECAUSE OF IMPROVEMENTS IN AIRPORT INFRASTRUCTURE, IN NAVIGATIONAL AIDS AND ABOVE ALL THE RELIABILITY OF ENGINES, THE COMMERCIAL OPERATION OF LARGE FLYING BOATS WAS GRADUALLY ABANDONED. SERIES PRODUCTION WAS LIMITED TO AIRCRAFT FOR RESCUE WORK, ANTI-SUBMARINE WARFARE, LIGHT TRANSPORT AND FIRE-FIGHTING.

The Convair YF2Y-1 Sea Dart raises a great cloud of spray on takeoff. This was the only seaplane to break the sound barrier.

The seaplane as a pleasure craft in the early sixties. A Lake LA-4 in attractive surroundings.

The SE-200 no.3 did not fly until after the war, and had less powerful engines than its competitor, the Laté 631, which was chosen by Air France.

L ong before the war, French official circles had been aware of the way their aircraft industry had been lagging behind in the field of transport flying boats. If the maxim is true that "a country enjoys the same esteem as its aviation industry", it became imperative to set in motion as quickly as possible a proper programme for the production of flying boats for transatlantic travel. The industry's technical service published a list of specifications for a commercial aircraft weighing 40 tons with a range of 3,750 miles against a headwind of 37mph, carrying 20 passengers provided with bunks, 1,100lb of cargo and a crew of six. These requirements applied to crossings of the North Atlantic, flying direct from France to the United States. Three constructors took up the challenge.

FRENCH TRANSATLANTIC FLYING BOATS

The disappointment

The Potez-CAMS 161 at Marignane.
This aircraft was used by the Germans up to 1944 for special missions.

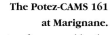

Potez-CAMS under the direction of Commander Hurel put forward a proposal for a flying boat, but before putting it into production they carried out a particularly elaborate test programme using a flying model to an approximately one-third scale. This Potez-CAMS 160, powered by six 40hp Train engines, took off in June 1938. These tests enabled some final alterations to be made to the Potez-CAMS 161, which was then already under construction. After numerous delays because of the Occupation and two changes of site for the assembly line, the Potez-CAMS 161 took off from a stretch of water at Sartrouville to touch down at Mureaux on March 20th 1942. After three flights, the 161 reached first Biscarosse and then Marignane. The moment the demarcation line was crossed, Commander Hurel was surprised to see the German navigator opening a bottle of champagne to celebrate the event! From Marignane the 161 took off with a weight of 42 tons, but permission for endurance tests was not forthcoming from the German authorities, who had invaded the free zone.

Initially the Potez-CAMS 161 came under the technical

direction of Deutsche Lufthansa, represented by Werner von Engel. The German company was seriously considering opening new routes with the return of peace. The tests to assess the French machines were an opportunity to gather information at minimum cost. For their part, the military authorities, grasping the possibility that these aircraft could be used in the Atlantic, decided to bring them together on Lake Constance to convert them into warplanes. The Potez-CAMS was destroyed at its moorings by P-51 Mustangs.

The half-disappointment

Lioré et Olivier designed the LeO H.49, which became the SE 200 when the company merged with the S.N.C.A. Sud-Est. Powered by six 1,450hp Wright Super Cyclone engines, the SE 200 had a wing without any bracing, but with the wing floats fixed to it. The tail had two fins, which were quickly modified in the course of initial testing. On December 11th 1942, Jacques Lacarme, a graduate of the École polytechnique whose scientific rigour was only matched by his high moral principles, was responsible for the SE 200's maiden flight, just after the occupation of the southern zone. The tests lasted all year because of the shortage of aviation fuel and the restrictions imposed by the Germans, who were afraid that the flying boats would reach the liberated territories of North Africa. Finally on January 17th 1944, in spite of the risks of sabotage, SE 200-01 left Marignane with an all-German aircrew. However, due to von Engel's conciliatory attitude, none of the prototypes was damaged by the Resistance. SE 200-01 then sank on April 17th 1944 on Lake Constance after being bombed by two Mosquitoes.

The second SE-200 was completely destroyed in 1944 when it was crushed by the main roof girder of its hangar in a bombing raid.

SE 200-02 was damaged by the main girder of the big hangar at Marignane on March 10th 1944 during a devastating bombing raid on the S.N.C.A.S.E. factory. Luckily the third example had not suffered too much, and was able to fly on May 2nd 1946. The Latécoère 631 having been chosen in May 1944 by the provisional government in Algiers for series production, the SE 200-03 had to make do with 1,200hp Gnome-Rhône 14 R engines, the more powerful Wright engines being reserved for the Latécoère. These underpowered engines ruined the aircraft, which was used when new as a backdrop for a fashion parade in Marseilles harbour or as the pretext for a visit by the Air Minister, Charles Tillon. On July 21st 1946 it made a symbolic flight to Germany, where it touched down on Lake Constance after flying over the submerged wreck of its elder brother. About the same time, it took part in the Villacoublay air show, flying so low that, to quote the pilot, Jacques Lacarme, "the crowd drew back like waves parted by the hull".

SE 200-03 went to the *Centre d'essais en vol* (Flight Testing

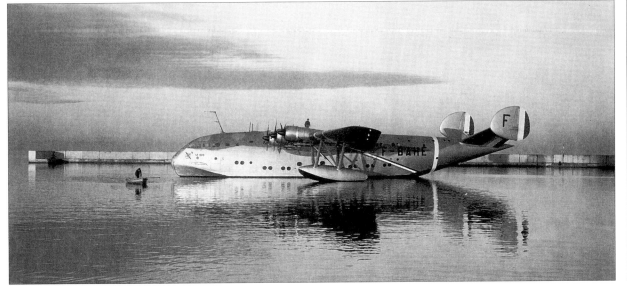
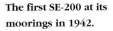

The first SE-200 at its moorings in 1942. The upper surfaces of the aircraft are painted in a makeshift camouflage.

The Laté 631 was the only six-engined flying boat in the world to be used on commercial routes.

F-BDRC was to crash into the sea on August 4th 1948.

The fifth Laté 631 was used by Air France and then by the S.E.M.A.F. in Africa.

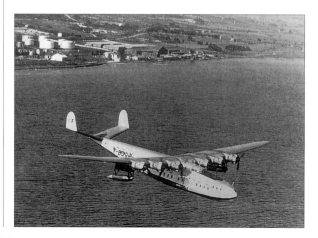

Centre). Its large size made it an unusual aircraft, with which a great variety of equipment could usefully be tested, engines assessed and aircrews trained. Its endurance of more than 15 hours was another point in its favour. On October 18th 1949, the pilot Jean Sarrail had to put an officer from the naval air arm (who hated the water!) through his pilot's test in a flying boat. The flight ended with a dive into the Étang de Berre, the aircraft – in submarine style – scraping the bottom which was fortunately not at all deep, and re-emerging. Sarrail cut the engines when the terrified pilot tried to take off again.

Once the damage had been repaired, SE 200-03 made some further flights, before being abandoned and then scrapped. SE 200-04, which was 93% complete, lay close to the Marignane air terminal until the mid-60s. SE 200-01 was fished out of the waters of Lake Constance without any particular care, so there was nothing left of it.

After the war, it was planned to build a giant flying boat of 140 tons. The SE 1200 would have had the same general lines as the SE 200, but with four much more powerful engines and a greatly improved aerodynamic shape, since for the first time both the floats and the step would have been retractable. The S.N.C.A.S.E. built a scale model of the projected machine, fitted with four 300hp engines. Jacques Lacarme made about 40 flights in this from June 1948 onwards, and all its innovative features were proved, but there was no future for the giant flying boat.

The half-success

On November 4th 1942 the Laté 631-01 made its first flight at Marignane. It was the largest and the heaviest of the three flying boats answering the 1936 specification. Its construction was interrupted by the war and was not taken up again until after the armistice. Assembly took place in a hangar at Marignane, not far from that of the S.N.C.A.S.E.

The test flights were completed in spite of the political difficulties described above; they showed that the 631 possessed excellent flying and seaworthiness qualities, and that the performance figures fulfilled the requirements. However, momentary vibrations at the extremities of the wings were noted. On January 21st 1944 the aircraft reached Lake Constance, where it was sunk at the same time as the SE 200-01.

The second Laté 631 flew on March 7th 1945 in spite of the difficulties experienced by the firm, which was accused of collaborating with the enemy. Although unquestionably a success, the flying boat, christened *Lionel de Marmier*, posed a number of problems connected with its 1,450hp Wright engines, and several items of equipment had to be revised. Notwithstanding the reservations of the constructor and of the C.E.V., the Air Minister Charles Tillon decided that overseas flights should be made.

On July 31st the aircraft accordingly made a flight of 3,760 miles from Biscarosse to Dakar, a distance equivalent to a North Atlantic crossing. The return was on August 4th. On October 10th a demonstration in South America ended with the hull being ripped open over a length of 20 feet as a result of hitting a block of concrete. Thirteen days later, the Laté, with 80 passengers on board, made a stopover at Port Étienne (Nouhadibou), then crossed the South Atlantic. On October 31st the propeller blades of the port inboard engine came off in flight and sliced into the hull, killing two passengers. Even so, the flying boat continued its demonstration flights on February 16th 1946, before returning to Biscarosse on March 6th. This tour created a disastrous mistrust of the Laté 631, at a time when 11 aircraft had already been built.

However, Air France bought four of them, fitted out to carry 46 passengers. On July 25th 1947 the third 631, christened *Guillaumet*, began a commercial service to the West Indies. This use lasted just one year, since on August 1st 1948 the sixth machine disappeared in the West Indies with 58 passengers on board. Air France then decided to dispose of these flying boats, which were too unreliable and were no longer economic as

SE-200 no.3, seen overflying the Étang de Berre, spent three years with the Centre d'essais en vol, which explains the presence of roundels and the civil registration F-BAIY on the wings.

153

compared with the contemporary landplanes.

A third 631 was lost in a storm near Barneville-Carteret on February 21st 1948, which left four machines available with four more to come. The Société d'exploitation des matériels aéronautiques français (S.E.M.A.F.) decided to use the Latés for transporting cotton in Africa. From November 1949 they used the fifth aircraft, but the results were not commercially satisfactory. The third 631, which was returning to Africa, went down at sea on March 28th 1950 as a result of aerodynamic flutter. The Laté 631s were then banned from flying, which led to the collapse of S.E.M.A.F., whose African activities were taken over by France Hydro. The eighth 631 carried a total of 3,300 tons of cotton between Lake Léré in Tchad and Douala in Cameroun. A final accident on September 10th 1955, although attributable to the weather conditions, finally put an end to the use of the Laté 631.

THE BIGGEST OF THEM ALL

"If this flying boat fails to fly, I'll leave the country."

Howard Hughes hurled this phrase at the journalists who were following him. How would the crazy venture end on which the Californian millionaire had embarked on November 16th 1942? On that date, the shipbuilder Henry J. Kaiser formed a company with Howard Hughes which was to produce three giant transport flying boats, made entirely of spruce wood in order to save metal for other uses. The engines, the propellers and the instruments were supplied by the U.S. Navy. The contract amounted to 18 million dollars. The construction of the HK-1 Hercules ran into such difficulties that work on it was finally abandoned in February 1944. President Roosevelt intervened personally to

ensure that at least one example should be completed after all. Henry Kaiser parted company with Howard Hughes, who renamed the flying boat H-4.

The flight of the Hercules

The aircraft, built at Culver City, California, was of monstrous size: 218ft 6ins long with a wingspan of 320ft 6ins, it weighed more than 181 tons on takeoff. No fewer than 700 soldiers could be accommodated in its fuselage. The motive power was provided by eight 3,000hp Pratt & Whitney R4360 Wasp Majors, the most powerful engines available at the time.

The main difficulties to be overcome related to the gluing of the outer skin and the perfecting of the partially assisted flying controls. In 1946 the separate parts were transported 30 miles to Long Beach, where the Hercules was assembled. In July 1947 Howard Hughes came before a Senate committee which accused him of having spent public money pointlessly on a machine incapable of flying. It was then that the millionaire, cut to the quick, uttered his famous phrase.

On November 1st the H-4 was launched, and the next day it was towed towards the sea with a crowd of journalists on board. The reporters disembarked again after sampling the handling qualities of the flying boat on the water. Howard Hughes, alone at the controls, began a high-speed taxiing run. At 90mph the aircraft, instead of slowing as planned, continued to accelerate; it lifted off, settling at about 70 feet above the water for approximately a mile before coming down onto the water again.

On the shore, the enthusiastic but baffled spectators expected some explanation from Howard Hughes, but none was

The Hughes H-4 taxiing in Los Angeles Bay on November 2nd 1947.
The H-4 remains the largest flying boat in history.

The presence of Howard Hughes in the pilot's seat gives an impression of the enormous size of the Hercules.

On November 2nd 1947 the Hughes H-4 makes its one and only flight, remaining airborne for about a mile. Howard Hughes himself piloted the giant flying boat.

forthcoming. The most likely hypothesis is that the flying boat began to pitch dangerously at high speed, and the pilot decided to take off in order to stop the movement. The feelings of euphoria which Hughes displayed in front of the press did not impress the specialist journalists.

Back before the Senate committee, Howard Hughes wore a triumphant smile. He was cleared of having squandered public money. The complaint was all the more unjust in that he had himself financed the final stages of the work. Hughes almost immediately lost interest in the Hercules, which was destined never to fly again.

In fact the basic concept could no longer be justified in 1947, whereas it had seemed attractive five years earlier. As with all his aircraft, Howard Hughes took trouble to preserve the H-4 in the best possible conditions. After his death the Spruce Goose Museum at Long Beach was opened to the public. Later on the machine was removed to Seattle to free up the museum site for developers, who little cared for one of the most beautiful creations of the age of the flying boat.

THE LAST COMMERCIAL FLYING BOATS

The U.S. Navy did not wait for the war to end in order to return the flying boat transports which it had requisitioned. Pan Am

considered them very out of date and was no longer using them, as the landplane had taken the place of the flying boat on transoceanic routes.

In 1946 Universal Airlines acquired seven Boeing 314s, reselling five of them to American International. These seven surviving aircraft, three of which came from B.O.A.C. (British Overseas Airways Corporation), flew in 1948 in the colours of World Airways, but at the end of 1949 they were taken out of service. The famous Clippers ended up as scrap.

In order to compete with the Boeing 314, the Vought-Sikorsky combine created the VS-44, a commercial adaptation of the sea patrol flying boat XPBS-1, which had remained at the prototype stage in spite of the excellent flying performance it had shown from August 1937 onward.

Three examples of the VS-44A were produced for American Export Airlines, and the first, named *Excalibur*, flew for the first time on January 18th 1942. In June 1942 A.E.A. inaugurated a transatlantic service, but *Excalibur* sank at its moorings several months later, in October. *Exeter*, the second production aircraft, was lost in August 1947 in Uruguay. *Excambian* remained as the sole survivor. In 1957 it was taken into service again, carrying 47 passengers from Long Beach to Avalon Bay on Catalina Island. After 10 years of operation, it was sold to Antilles Air Boat.

The Vought-Sikorsky VS-44 was the last commercial flying boat designed by Sikorsky. *Excalibur*, the first of the three built, sank eight months after its maiden flight.

Damaged in 1969, the last transatlantic flying boat was rescued by an American museum.

In Britain, Short had already adapted some Sunderland Mk 3s as transports. From 1945 on B.O.A.C. used 28 of these flying boats. The Sandringham was revised for civil operation, with improvements to the hull and the nose, which was rounded off as the front turret and its mounting were eliminated. The prototype flew in November 1945, and 18 production examples left the works. They were used by overseas companies in Tasmania, Norway and the West Indies, while B.O.A.C. operated them in the Far East. In 1958, when most of them had been taken out of service, the Réseau aérien interinsulaire (R.A.I. or Inter-island Air Network) bought one to provide links between the islands of French Polynesia. This aircraft's last flight, when it was piloted by Douglas Pearson, took place in September 1970; it also marked the end of the use of flying boats by French commercial airlines. The last flying boat derived from Short military aircraft was the S.45 Solent, the civil version of the Seaford (developed from the Sunderland IV). A production run of 18 was made with Bristol Hercules engines giving 1,700hp, or in two cases, 2,040hp. Aquila Airways brought the commercial operation of flying boats in Great Britain to an end on September 30th 1958.

The standardization of equipment, the improvement in the performance of landplanes and the low cost of creating rudimentary landing strips were all factors that contributed to the demise of the last survivors of the brief heyday of the large transport flying boats.

An R.A.I. publicity photo showing the role played by its Sandringham, which was to provide communications between the islands of French Polynesia.

The R.A.I.'s Short Sandringham at its moorings at Papeete in 1958, bearing the company's original colours.

157

The Saro Princess is so far the heaviest British aircraft to have flown,with a maximum weight of 149 tons.

The flicker of the contra-rotating propellers of the Saro Princess provides a most attractive effect.
Fitted with ten turboprop engines, the aircraft did not appeal to B.O.A.C., its first potential buyer.

THE SARO PRINCESS

At the end of the Second World War, the advent of new and much more powerful engines in the form of turbojets and turboprops paved the way for the design of larger and heavier aircraft. In July 1945, Saunders-Roe (or Saro) were commissioned to produce three examples of the SR.45 Princess, destined for B.O.A.C.

With a wingspan of 219ft 6ins and a length of 148ft, the Princess had a 'double bubble' fuselage which made it possible to pressurize the cabin efficiently for the 105 passengers to be carried in commercial operation. A lower section was divided into watertight compartments.

To propel this mass of 150 tons, the SR.45 had ten Bristol Proteus 600 turboprops, each providing 3,200hp and 800lb residual thrust. The eight inboard engines were coupled in pairs and drove contra-rotating propellers.

Since B.O.A.C. had already decided to stop using flying boats in November 1950, the launching of the Princess on August 20th 1952 came rather late in the day. The maiden flight was made two days later. The tests which followed showed that the gearboxes between the engines and the propellers were too weak, and the associated mechanical problems meant long hours of research. At a time when all countries were giving up the commercial use of flying boats, work of this kind could not be justified, even for a machine capable of reaching 370mph or more and flying for 15 hours.

The prototype ended its flights in 1954. It was preserved for a number of years, in the hope that it might be used again for experimental purposes. The project of providing it with atomic power came to nothing.

THE CONVAIR TRADEWIND

While the British were trying to perfect a commercial flying boat with turboprop engines, the Americans laid down a specification in 1945 for a patrol aircraft with this form of motive power. Although no propeller turbines had at the time proved themselves in flight, much was expected of them. Ten examples

The Convair R3Y-1 Tradewind taxiing in San Diego Bay immediately before its first flight on February 25th 1954.

of the Convair XP5Y-1 Tradewind were ordered in June 1946, and were intended to replace the Martin Mariner in the shorter or longer term. The hull had a length-to-beam ratio of ten to one like the Blohm und Voss BV 238, the length being nearly 142ft and the wingspan 145ft 9ins, much smaller dimensions than those of the German flying boat.

The turboprop engines caused such difficulties that Westinghouse abandoned work on them. As a replacement the U.S. Navy chose the Allison T40, made up of two Allison T38s driving contra-rotating propellers via two drive shafts connected to a single reduction gear.

The maiden flight of the Convair XP5Y-1 took place on April 18th 1950. In spite of innumerable problems with the engines, the flying boat set up an endurance record for a turboprop aircraft, flying for 8 hours in August 1950. The first XP5Y-1 crashed into the sea during a high-speed test on July 15th 1953 after completing only 102 flying hours. The second XP5Y-1 was only used for ground testing.

Meanwhile the U.S. Navy, satisfied with the P5M-1 Marlin, abandoned the patrol version in favour of a transport version as a backup for the Martin Mars in VR-2 Squadron. The first R3Y-1

flew on February 25th 1954. Another five followed, equipped with T40-A-10 engines delivering 5,330hp; they had an extended nose section incorporating a large side door for loading. The fourth R3Y-1 flew from San Diego to Patuxent River in six hours, crossing the United States at an average speed of 403mph, a record for a flying boat.

A final version, designated the R3Y-2, flew on October 22nd 1954. It fulfilled the role of an assault transport which could disembark on a beach three 155mm howitzers, two half-track vehicles or six jeeps. The nose could be opened, and access ramps made loading and unloading easier. The R3Y-2 could also carry 103 soldiers or evacuate 92 wounded in stretchers, accompanied by 12 medical attendants. Three R3Y-2s of the six made and one R3Y-1 were modified to provide in-flight refuelling of four fighters at the same time.

The first Tradewind went into service in March 1956 with VR-2 squadron, which was to take six in all. After two accidents (without any loss of life), flights by R3Ys were stopped in January 1958. None was preserved. The Tradewind, which had taken ten years to design and develop, was only in service for two years without staking a claim as compared with its land-based competitors. Its only original feature was the disembarkation facility, but the U.S. Navy gave it up as its priority was to finance its programme of atomic submarines armed with nuclear missiles.

THE JET FIGHTER SEAPLANES

The arrival on the aeronautical scene of the turbojet produced general euphoria in design studios. The ambition to produce a fighter seaplane capable of competing with land-based fighters was the motive for several projects. Only two were completed,

The R-3Y2 was distinguished from its predecessor in that its bow section, fitted with a radome, could be raised.

The Caribbean Tradewind is trailing a hose for in-flight refuelling.

With its unusual shape, the Saro SR.A/1 was unable to compete with the land-based fighters of its generation.

Carrier-borne aircraft were preferred to it.

The Saro SR.A/1, which flew in July 1947, made its mark in the history of the seaplane as the first to be jet-propelled.

these being the British Saro SR.A/1 and the American Convair XF2Y-1 Sea Dart.

The British Solution

The Saro SR.A/1 was the result of design work carried out from 1943 onward by the engineers Gouge and Knowler of Saro in conjunction with D.M. Smith of Metropolitan-Vickers, who developed in the utmost secrecy an axial-flow turbojet, the F 2/4, giving 3,230lb thrust. In May 1944 Saro received an order for three aircraft in accordance with the E.6/44 specification.

A twin-engined single-seater with a wingspan of 46ft and a length of 50ft, the SR.A/1 had an air intake high up in the bow so as to escape the spray. The wing floats were semi-retractable into the wings. It was the first aircraft to have an ejector seat made by Martin-Baker.

The first SR.A/1 made its maiden flight on July 16th 1947, and testing of it continued until June 1951. The second prototype crashed into the sea as a result of pilot error. The third was used for high-speed tests, reaching 498mph at 20,000 feet and Mach 0.82 in a dive on August 12th 1949. The legendary Eric Brown hit a tree trunk when touching down and owed his life to Geoffrey Tyson, the Saro chief pilot, who dived into the water fully clothed to rescue him. The loss of two prototypes in one month discouraged the authorities from investing in a machine with a limited performance. Further flights of the remaining prototype in 1950 and 1951 did nothing to change this decision.

A supersonic flying boat

The United States had considerable difficulty in developing jet engines. In the immediate postwar period they had to make use of British designs until they could make up the leeway. This is at least part of the reason why the U.S. Navy did not launch a programme for a jet fighter seaplane until October 1948. After testing hydroskis on various landplanes and amphibians, Convair produced a delta-wing aircraft which was fitted with two skis. It was adopted by the U.S. Navy, which ordered two of them in January 1951.

A delta-wing single-seater with a wingspan of 33ft 8ins and a length of 52ft 7ins, the Sea Dart had two Westinghouse J34-WE-32 turbojets, each delivering 3,400lb thrust. The XF2Y-1 made a flight of 300 yards on January 14th 1953, in the course of a hydrodynamic test, and flew properly on April 9th. The hydroskis, which vibrated dangerously, created enormous difficulties. Also the flying boat's aerodynamics prevented it from going supersonic in level flight. The use of Westinghouse J46-WE-2s giving 6,000lb thrust with afterburners improved its performance.

On August 3rd 1954 Charles Richbourg exceeded Mach 1 at an altitude of 34,000 feet in the second example, designated YF2Y-1. The Convair Sea Dart became the first supersonic seaplane, and remains to this day the only one to have achieved this feat. This YF2Y-1 then broke up during a demonstration flight on November 4th 1954. The U.S. Navy had already given up the idea of series production of the Sea Dart, and only four YF2Y-1s had been funded in addition to the XF2Y-1. Numerous tests were made to resolve the problems posed by the hydroskis. B.J. Long made tests using just one ski up to 1956. The Sea Dart showed that it could take off in waves up to 10 feet high, easily exceeding the requirements of the specification. On the other hand, when fitted with a hydrofoil it could not unstick itself from the water.

The concept of a jet fighter seaplane did not succeed in

The Convair YF2Y-1 is the only flying boat to have broken the sound barrier, which it did on August 3rd 1954. This aircraft exploded at a public demonstration on November 4th 1954, killing the pilot, Charles (Chuck) E. Richbourg.

The last tests of the Sea Dart were conducted on a small rigid hydroski, similar to a hydrofoil, with which it never succeeded in taking off.

offering any competition to the carrier-borne fighters. However those that were produced exert sufficient fascination for the Saro SR.A/1 and four Sea Darts to have been preserved, at a time when quite a number of prototypes ended up as scrap.

THE MASTER OF THE SEAS

Of all the flying boats built in the fifties, the Martin P6M Seamaster had the most ambitious specification. The U.S. Navy wanted a flying boat capable of flying at altitude at supersonic speeds, then descending when 100 miles from its target to 100 feet to escape the enemy radar, and dropping mines at over 600mph to block enemy ports before returning to its servicing ship. The machine was to be able spend six months in the water. It would be refuelled either in flight or by submarines. Martin's project was chosen in October 1952. Two XP6M-1s and six YP6M-1s were funded, plus 24 production P6M-2s.

The first XP6M-1 flew on July 14th 1955. It crashed on December 7th as a result of a breakage of the tailplane, causing the deaths of the four members of the crew. The second XP6M-1

flew on May 18th 1956. On December 9th the tailplane was again implicated in an accident, but this time the four members of the crew fortunately succeeded in making the first multiple ejection.

The first YP6M-1, equipped with Allison J71-A-4 turbojets giving 13,000lb thrust with afterburners, did not fly until January 20th 1958. The five others that followed in the course of the year showed themselves capable of reaching a maximum speed of 683mph (Mach 0.90) at sea level, a most remarkable performance compared with the B.52's Mach 0.55 in the same circumstances. While the orders for the production models kept on being reduced, the P6M-2 took off for the first time on February 17th 1959. The wing no longer had any dihedral, which took the load off the wing tip-mounted floats; the rotary bomb bay held up to 30,000lb of explosives, cameras for reconnaissance and even an in-flight refuelling installation. Fitted with four Pratt & Whitney J75-P-2 turbojets giving 17,500lb thrust, the P6M-2, with a takeoff weight of 188,000lb, could reach a speed of 723mph (Mach 0.95) at sea level. The speed range should have gone up to Mach 1.1

The first Martin P6M-2 at liftoff. It was the best performer of all the combat seaplanes, with a speed range up to Mach 1.1.

at altitude, but the tests were stopped on August 21st 1959 when only three P6M-2s had flown. Altogether the Seamaster had clocked up 536 flying hours.

The reasons for giving up an aircraft with such an excellent performance were many. Certainly, it put the bombers of the U.S.A.F. at a disadvantage by proving that a flying boat could perform better than the landplanes, but above all it was because – between the programme launch and production – the priorities had changed in favour of financing nuclear submarines equipped with Polaris missiles. Also the admirals, whose experience was of carrier-borne flying, preferred conventional shipboard aircraft to seaplanes.

All the Seamasters were destroyed, as well as all the documents relating to them, as if there were a desire to remove all trace of them and thus ensure that the dubious nature of the decision to abandon the project from a technical point of view could not be examined in future.

While the Seamaster was consigned to oblivion, Western observers were surprised in 1961 to discover four Beriev Be-10 twin-jet flying boats airborne at Tushino Air Show near Moscow.

The second P6M-2 seen from the front shows that the air intakes are set well back in comparison with the earlier versions to prevent the spray being sucked in.

According to legend, the cradle used for manoeuvring the P6M-1 on the ground cost just as much as a Seamaster, which was wrong, as was the financial assessment of the programme which led to its cancellation.

1946. The seaplanes were no exception to this rule: the Laté 298s, Loire 130s and Laté 611s were mixed with Dornier Do 24s, Catalinas and Sunderlands, not forgetting the Nakajima A6M2-N Rufes and Aichi E13A1 Jakes based at Saigon. The Breguet 730s and 731s, which became available in 1944, had not played any part in the war.

In the following period, only the Nord 1402 Noroît, a twin-engined multi-purpose amphibian, was designed in France and 25 were made. Coming into service in 1951, it was dropped by the French Navy four years later because its engines were unreliable.

The sea rescue Dornier Do 24s were taken out of service the same year. The Supermarine Sea Otter replaced the Loire 130s in Indochina, where they notched up numerous surveillance missions on the rivers until they were replaced in turn by the Grumman JRF-6 Goose, which remained on the strength until 1962.

No fewer than 54 Short Sunderlands were used by the French Navy from 1943 to 1961, giving way to Martin P5M-2 Marlins, 10 of which were delivered to Dakar in 1959. After five accident-free years, nine machines returned to the United States, the tenth being used as a source of spare parts. By October 1st

The Nord 1402 Noroît was the last military seaplane built in France.

The Dornier Do 24 was produced at Sartouville after the war for air-sea rescue missions.
It was in service until 1954.

Beriev was the designer of the first Russian jet-propelled flying boat, the R-1, which flew in May 1952. The Be-10 had no better luck than its American counterpart, never getting beyond the prototype stage. On the other hand, it did set up a series of world records for seaplanes.

THE LAST MILITARY SEAPLANES IN FRANCE
In common with all the other French military forces, the naval air arm had a very mixed bag of equipment at the end of the war, as is shown by the list of machines on the strength at January 1st

As part of the American aid programme, this Martin P5M-2 Marlin was assigned to Squadron 27F at Dakar for five years.

1964 the naval air arm no longer had a single seaplane. It was an irony of fate that the old Catalina, which had been assigned to 6F Squadron in 1943 and had carried the hook roundel until 1958, reappeared in 1965 to undertake aid missions at the Centre d'experimentation du Pacifique. Three PBY-5As fulfilled this role until December 1971, this great machine finally bringing to a close the era of water-based aviation in the French naval air arm.

THE MARLIN, LAST AMERICAN PATROLLER

On May 30th 1948, Martin flew a Mariner with an entirely redesigned hull, the aim being to improve its seaworthiness. It was lengthened considerably, and had hydroflaps at the rear which enabled it to manoeuvre more easily in the water. After 18 months of tests, a new machine with numerous validated improvements was ordered by the U.S. Navy. The P5M-1 had 3,250hp Wright Cyclone R3350-30W engines, behind which were placed two bomb racks. Altogether 167 P5M-1s left the Martin

factories, and the first aircraft flew on June 22nd 1951. It entered service on April 23rd 1952. A few were allocated to the Coast Guard and were specially equipped for rescue missions. A new version, designated P5M-2, became operational on April 29th 1954. The hull had been further refined so that it could lift off cleanly on takeoff. The tailplane was placed at the top of the tail fin in order to be clear of the spray. The anti-submarine equipment was completely revised.

The last of the 119 P5M-2s was delivered to the U.S. Navy on December 20th 1960. Redesignated SP-5B in 1962, the Marlin played its part in the surveillance of the Vietnamese coast from 1964 onward as part of the operation "Market Time", which it carried out for three years, responding to the gunfire of the Vietcong ships supplying the troops in the Mekong Delta. The advent of the Lockheed P-3A Orion marked the end of the era of

The Marlin's ability to manoeuvre on the water was greatly improved by the fitting of flaps operating as a rudder. The circle traced by the P5M-1's wake is remarkably tight considering the size of this flying boat.

Group flight by P5M-1 Marlins belonging to VP-56 Squadron. The Marlin was the U.S. Navy's last patrol flying boat.

The Grumman UF-1s never served in specially formed units as did the U.S.A.F.'s Albatrosses. They played a support role as a personnel transport and rescue aircraft, operating from the bases to which they were attached.

Twelve Albatrosses were modified by Grumman for use as passenger transports. N112FB, seen here at liftoff, was used for the certification of the G-111. Its first flight took place on February 13th 1979.

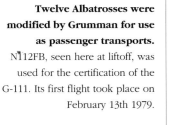

the American patrol flying boats. In May 1967 VP-40 Squadron completed its last mission with Marlins. Five months later one example left San Diego in California for the Patuxent River, Maryland, where it was stored before taking its place in the Naval Aviation Museum.

SO THAT OTHERS MAY LIVE

Heir to a long line of twin-engined amphibious flying boats, the Grumman Albatross was the last flying boat to see service in numerous countries; air-sea rescue missions were increasingly undertaken by helicopters, which had become sufficiently reliable from 1965 on.

The Good Samaritan

Ordered in 1944, the XJR2F-1 did not fly until October 1st 1947, having survived the postwar cuts in the American military budget. Curiously, the U.S. Air Force, which had just been created, was much more interested in the aircraft than the U.S. Navy. The test flights showed that the amphibian, 62ft 1in long with a wingspan of 80ft, could fly at 236mph and had a range of 2,200 miles by virtue of its two 1,425hp Wright R1820-76A engines. The U.S.A.F. got production under way by taking over an order placed by the U.S. Navy, and in this way acquired 290 examples of the SA-16A, with which it equipped all its rescue units. The U.S. Navy bought 99 of the similar UF-1s, fitted out as transports, and the U.S. Coast Guard received 86 UF-1Gs.

In the Korean War the Albatross crews recorded some remarkable feats, competing in daring with the helicopter pilots to rescue wounded men from enemy lines. For instance, on June 11th 1951 Lieutenant Najarian put his SA-16A down on the Taedong River by the light of Mustang beacons. He picked up Captain Stewart and left again without showing any concern about the darkness, the shallow water, drifting objects, electric cables, or the anti-aircraft fire from the bank. For this action he received the highest distinction awarded in time of war to a pilot in the Air Rescue Service. Many similarly heroic actions were not recognized in this war, in particular the setting down and picking up of agents behind enemy lines.

Grumman improved their amphibian by modifying it so that it could land on and take off from snow. It thus became a 'triphibian'. In spite of its remarkable hydrodynamic qualities and an exceptional safety rating, the Albatross did have some faults. Grumman therefore extended the wingspan by 16ft 8ins, removed the radio masts and modified the wing profile, which made it possible to fly the aircraft on one engine without losing altitude, to lower the stalling speed and to increase the range by more than 500 miles, without increasing the power of the engines.

On the other hand its seagoing qualities were impaired by the removal of the wing floats. The new version received the designation SA-16B in the U.S.A.F. and UF-2 in the U.S. Navy. The first SA-16B flew on January 16th 1956, and altogether 91 SA-16As were converted, while 31 UF-1s became UF-2s. For its part the U.S. Coast Guard updated its 81 Albatrosses into UF-2Gs.

A universal flying boat

The American air forces had ordered Albatrosses in massive quantities when the Korean War was at its height. The very low rate of losses and the large numbers produced soon led to the delivery of secondhand examples as part of the military aid programme.

Altogether 20 countries acquired Albatrosses, in most cases as replacements for Catalinas. Portugal received the first batch in 1954, Germany took delivery of eight from 1958 on, Spain became the largest recipient with 26 aircraft, Italy used a dozen SA-16As for 20 years, while Greece was the last country to use them, its Albatrosses going into well-deserved retirement in 1995.

In order to increase the versatility of their amphibian, Grumman developed a version for anti-submarine warfare which retained all its other facilities. The first SHU-16Bs arrived in Norway in 1961. The 36 SHU-16Bs made were all conversions of existing airframes, and served in five countries. In 1962 the

Americans adopted a unified system of designations: the U.S.A.F.'s SA-16As and SA-16Bs became HU-16As and HU-16Bs, the U.S. Navy's UF-1s and UF-2s became HU-16Cs and HU-16Ds, while the U.S. Coast Guard's UF-2Gs received the designation HU-16E.

In June 1964 some HU-16Bs arrived in South Vietnam. They were used as aerial command posts for rescue operations and to pick up crews who had gone down in the Gulf of Tonkin. They were progressively replaced by the HC-130H Hercules and by helicopters, which were much more suitable. Their last wartime mission was on September 30th 1967. Altogether the Albatrosses had rescued 147 flyers and picked up some 20 agents behind enemy lines. Four aircraft were lost, two of them in combat.

The U.S.A.F. kept its last HU-16Bs until 1973. For its part, the U.S. Navy, which had not used them in Vietnam, finally gave them up in 1976. The U.S. Coast Guard, which appreciated its endurance of 16 hours and its low speed for patrol duties, used its HU-16Es until 1983.

Realizing that of the 464 Albatrosses built a large number could be restored to flying condition with a few modifications, Grumman offered a civil version for carrying 28 passengers. The first G-111 flew in February 1979, but only the oldest American airline, Chalk's, bought a dozen aircraft. The Smithsonian Institution acquired two, as did the Malaysians. Production stopped at this point, but thanks to Chalk's who were still using them in 1996, and to a few collectors, the Albatrosses will still be flying in the 21st century.

Some of the HU-16Bs which were deployed in Vietnam were given a strange grey-blue livery. The Albatrosses gave way to the helicopters.

In 1962, the UF-2G 7255 set up a whole series of records for a flying boat of its class, including a straight-line flight of 3,570 miles.

167

The Shin-Meiwa US-1 was delivered to the Japanese Navy on March 4th 1975 as a replacement for the Grumman UF-2 Albatrosses in Kokutai 51.

The problem caused by spray thrown up by the four propellers of the PS-1's turboprops was resolved by placing the cockpit a long way forward, and by reducing the takeoff and landing distance.

THE REVIVAL OF JAPANESE FLYING BOATS

During the Second World War, Kawanishi had produced the best flying boat of its generation, the H8K-2. In 1949 the firm became Shin Meiwa and specialized in the maintenance of Japanese and American civil and military aircraft. The Japanese Navy's Self-Defence Force took delivery of six Grumman UF-2 Albatrosses, which were used for sea rescue missions. In October 1960 Shin Meiwa acquired a UF-1 designated UF-XS. The amphibian was to serve as a flying testbed for a short takeoff and landing aircraft designed by Shizuo Kikuhara, who had been responsible for the Mavis and Emily.

Since the most critical phases for the airframes of flying boats and their pilots are when taking off and touching down, Kikuhara like most of the aircraft constructors of the time endeavoured to reduce them to a minimum. The UF-XS was fitted with two 1,000hp General Electric T58 turbines feeding a boundary layer control system blowing air on the flaps in the trailing edge of the wing. The aircraft became a four-engined machine and was provided with a T tail as well as a very sophisticated hull.

The UF-XS made its maiden flight on December 20th 1962. Shin Meiwa undertook a first series of tests in the sheltered waters of Konan before delivering the aircraft to the Omura Kokutai, which took over for open-sea testing from December 14th 1963. The results were up to expectations and the career of the UF-XS continued until the PS-1 was ready to fly.

This time, in order to build a flying boat for anti-submarine warfare, Shin Meiwa used the Martin Marlin as a model. Fitted with four 2,850hp General Electric T64-IHI-10 turboprops, plus a T58-GE-10 turbine, the PS-1 had a length of 109ft 9ins and a wingspan of 108ft 9ins. The wing had a device for blowing on the flaps running along almost the whole of the trailing edge, acting also on the control surfaces (rudder and elevator). The air flow from the propellers helped to increase lift at low speeds. The hull, with just one step, had two deflectors in the bow which reduced the amount of spray thrown up. A tricycle undercarriage allowed low-speed manoeuvring on the ground, but it was not possible to take off and land the aircraft on a runway with this.

Tactical equipment comprised a search radar, a magnetic anomaly detection system, active and passive search buoys, and explosives mounted on the wing. Five operation posts were provided in a compartment at the back of the pilot's cabin. The PS-1 had above all the advantage that it could alight on the water in order to 'listen in' to the movements of submarines, and hence to pinpoint their positions with great accuracy.

The prototype of the PS-1 made its first flight on October 29th 1967. A second prototype joined it at Iwakuni as part of a detachment of Kokutai 51 to undergo operational tests. In 1969 Shin Meiwa were authorized to start assembly line production. The first production example flew on February 19th 1972. Kokutai 31, created on March 1st 1973, was given 23 PS-1s, the last being delivered in October 1979.

In the 1980s the development of electronic anti-submarine warfare equipment meant that the use of flying boats was no longer justified. Kokutai 31 was disbanded in 1989, giving way to Lockheed P-3C Orions.

Shin Meiwa offered the Japanese Navy an amphibious version, designated US-1, to replace the Grumman UF-2 Albatrosses. Optimized for search and rescue at sea, the US-1 had proper landing gear. The cabin normally contained 12 stretchers, but could take up to 36. Launchers for distress rockets, kits for survival at sea and life rafts made up the main rescue equipment.

A loudspeaker mounted in the tail fin made it possible to communicate with the survivors. To improve visibility, the US-1 was provided with large blister-shaped portholes. The crew of 12 men included two medical attendants and three rescue divers.

The US-1 made its first flight on October 18th 1974. It joined Kokutai 51 for operational assessment, then Kokutai 71 was created on July 1st 1976 at Iwakuni. In 1981 the base at Atsugi received a permanent transfer of three aircraft. Having delivered six US-1s, Shin Meiwa then produced nine US-1As which had more efficient electronic equipment. The flying boats were made part of a network, only stepping in where an operation was a long distance from the coast; they would fly to objectives up to 2,500 miles from their base, being refuelled en route. The ability to alight in wave troughs more than 12 feet deep was a considerable advantage which made it possible to operate in the north-western Pacific for almost the whole year, as opposed to only a quarter of the time with conventional flying boats.

Although it only performed about 40 missions a year, the Shin Meiwa US-1s and US-1As played a role that the helicopters could not undertake. These descendants of the Emily maintained the tradition of the great four-engined flying boats.

CANADAIR

For any industrial company, to see the name of its product identified with the function that it performs must indeed be a

The first US-1 has just lowered its large flaps on the trailing edge of the wing, the outer part of which has air blown on it. Their purpose was to reduce takeoff and landing speed.

The Shin Meiwa PS-1, which flew for the first time on October 29th 1967, had anti-submarine missions as its main role.

source of satisfaction as great as it is rare.

In 1985 the Canadair public relations manager told me with undisguised pride that the firm's name had just been given a dictionary entry, so that Canadair is defined as meaning a fire-fighting aircraft. This popular usage paid tribute to 20 years of efforts to establish the last civil flying boat in series production, the Canadair CL-215.

A unique aircraft

In 1963 the United States and Canada together produced a list of specifications for an aircraft to replace the landplanes and seaplanes used in the fight against the forest fires which ravage both California and the vast uninhabited tracts of Canada. Until then surplus machines from the Second World War had been used for this task, to which they were ill suited, exposing their crews to considerable risks. Only the Martin Mars offered a really efficient solution with its ability to drop 5,000 gallons of water, but there was no question of resuming production of this huge flying boat.

The design studies were for a twin-engined amphibian capable, like the Mars, of scooping up water from the surface in order to make several drops in a short period. The basic parameters required, in order that the mission should be completed with an adequate safety margin, were good stability when flying over the heat generated by the flames, a high degree of manoeuvrability at low altitude and excellent visibility for the pilot.

The Canadair firm based in Quebec decided to go ahead with the construction of the CL-215 in February 1966, having obtained guarantees of purchase from the French Protection Civile service (10 aircraft) and the Province of Quebec (20 aircraft).

On October 23rd 1967 the CL-215 made its maiden flight from the Cartierville runway. After final tests, the Protection Civile received its first three amphibians in June 1969. The Canadair gained a fine reputation the following year after its intensive use against the fires which ravaged the Côte d'Azur. Efficiency does not however mean freedom from risk, and on July 4th a Canadair crashed after touching the tops of trees hidden by dense black smoke.

The deaths of the three crew members did not reflect either on the aircraft or the procedure used. Altogether the Protection Civile acquired 15 aircraft, four of which were lost in accidents. Due to legal wrangles concerning the engines, the Province of Quebec did not receive its first machine until January 1970. The original order for 20 was reduced to 15.

Sales were soon limited by the closure of the American markets, where the regulations in force were unfavourable to the civil operation of seaplanes. Canadair was consequently obliged to restrict its production to 65 aircraft in 11 years, which

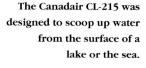

The Canadair CL-215 was designed to scoop up water from the surface of a lake or the sea.

The CL-215 in action.
The management of the Canadian firm derived much satisfaction from the fact that 'Canadair' had become a synonym for 'fire-fighting aircraft'.

Externally similar to the 415, this Spanish CL-215T belongs to the older generation as it does not have the adjustable, computer-controlled water-bombing facility, which doubled the work output of the CL-415 in comparison with its predecessor.

Family photo at the Quebec Air Service: an old Canso poses with a CL-215 and a CL-415.

increased their unit cost. Spain and Greece were the only countries to buy more than 10 aircraft.

They were also used for air-sea rescue missions, eight CL-215s ordered by Spain being fitted with weather and search radar. Thailand bought two identical examples without fire-fighting equipment. A Venezuelan transport company took two aircraft fitted with 26 passenger seats. In Canada the provinces of Ontario and Manitoba acquired two and three of them respectively. Production ceased in August 1982, at which time 74 had been built. The last examples were delivered to Yugoslavia and Italy.

Canadair decided to give events a helping hand. While for reasons of cost a number of countries continued to use secondhand aircraft for fire-fighting, an agreement between the firm and the Canadian government enabled production to be resumed in an entirely new factory at Dorval. Basing their argument on a report showing the scale of the economic disaster that would be caused in the medium term by the destruction of the Canadian forest by fire, the firm succeeded in obtaining an order from the Provinces for 35 Canadairs, which enabled them to cover the costs of production and to stabilize export prices.

Canadair was also able to plan a new version equipped with turboprop engines, the CL-215T, which got over the difficulty of providing petrol supplies. The very last CL-215, the 123rd, fitted with 2,100hp Pratt & Whitney R2800 engines, was delivered to Greece on May 3rd 1990.

The second generation

To widen its customer base, Canadair started by offering to convert the original CL-215s into CL-215Ts fitted with Pratt & Whitney 123 AF turboprops for a very competitive price. Two aircraft destined for Quebec were modified as CL-215T prototypes, the first making its maiden flight on June 8th 1989. It was given its certificate in 1991, and 15 aircraft were then modified in 1995, Canadair producing the structural parts and the engine nacelles which were then supplied to the De Havilland Canada factory in Toronto for assembly with the Pratt & Whitney turboprop engines.

The CL-415 represented the definitive version of the Canadair. An order for 12 examples on June 28th 1991 by the French enabled the programme to be launched in October of the same year. Canadair produced a first batch of 25 CL-415s, eight of which were destined for Quebec and four for Italy.

With a wingspan of 93ft 11ins and a length of 65ft, the CL-415 can carry 6 tons of water in tanks situated at the aircraft's centre of gravity. Fire-retardant products can be mixed with the water, which is poured from four trap doors opening in the bottom of the flying boat's hull. Two openings in the hull serve to scoop up the water required either from the surface of a lake or from the sea.

For a typical mission, the amphibian takes off from its base for an incident up to 100 miles away. A stretch of water about 12 miles from the fire enables it to scoop up and drop 6 tons of water 25 times before having to return to its base. The machine needs a distance of 1,400 yards to scoop up the maximum amount of water.

The fitting of the 2,380hp turboprop engines, which are much lighter than the piston engines, caused problems of trim. Canadair took the opportunity to improve the stability of the CL-215T and CL-415 by mounting slats at the ends of the wing and on the tailplane parallel to the tail fin. Certain flight commands

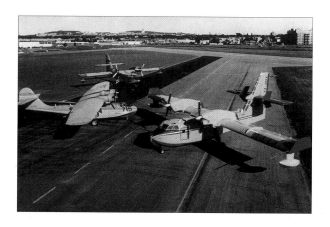

are hydraulically assisted, and in the pilot's cockpit, which is now air-conditioned, the crew have the benefit of an instrument panel provided with display screens.

The maximum speed of the CL-415 is 233mph, rate of climb is 23ft per second, and 'water-bombing' is carried out at 78mph. As compared with the original version, the CL-415 has an endurance of half an hour more with an identical fuel consumption, but at half the cost.

The CL-415 made its first flight on December 6th 1993. The first production example was officially delivered to France in April 1994, but after several modifications it finally arrived at Marignane on June 11th 1995. The CL-415s did not become fully operational until 1996.

One of a kind and extremely effective in carrying out its task, the Canadair remains the only flying boat in series production in the world today.

PAST OR FUTURE?

During the 1980s the name Dornier cropped up again in the world of seaplanes. A Dornier Do 24, bought by the Spanish in 1971, was given a new wing fitted with three 1,125hp PT6A-45B turboprop engines. Purely experimental, the Do 24TT flew for the first time on April 25th 1983. The test flights that followed showed that the aircraft had useful short takeoff and landing capabilities.

On August 18th 1984 the Claudius Dornier company, which had broken away from the parent company, presented the CD.1, the prototype of the amphibian Seastar transport. After tests on the water, which justified the construction of the CD.2, made entirely of composite materials, the aircraft made its first flight on April 24th 1987.

Provided with two 650hp PT6A-135A engines in tandem and

the famous lateral fins or sponsons, it was designed to carry 12 passengers 620 miles. The two examples were tested together for certification. Unfortunately there turned out to be no market for them, and the Dornier Composite Aircraft company went bankrupt in July 1991.

The most daring flying boat remains the Beriev A-40 Albatros. This superb amphibian, heir of a long line of Beriev military machines, flew in December 1986. Its role is to test technological innovations, such as the engine nacelles mounted behind the wings and containing the main landing gear. The A-40 flying boat beat 14 world records and, above all, it made possible the development of the Be-42, which is devoted to research and sea rescue. A veritable flying hospital, it contains equipment for treating 20 survivors for hypothermia at the same time. The Albatros has accommodation for 54 shipwreck victims. Intended for export, it is the only large amphibian aircraft still available and the last to compete with the air-sea rescue landplanes and helicopters.

Seagoing test for the Claudius Dornier CD.1 Seastar.
This flying boat is made entirely of composite materials.

A surprise at the 1991 Le Bourget Air Show was the presence of the highly spectacular Beriev A-40 Albatros, which unlike the Seamaster is an amphibian whose use is officially restricted to maritime search and rescue missions.

CHAPTER 6

Seaplane Paradise

IN SOME PARTS OF THE WORLD, SUCH AS THE WEST INDIES, ALASKA, AND WESTERN CANADA, SEAPLANES STILL PLAY AN IMPORTANT ROLE IN PASSENGER AND FREIGHT TRANSPORT. RALPH EVAIN HAS DEVOTED TEN YEARS OF HIS LIFE TO PHOTOGRAPHING THEM IN THESE AREAS, RIGHTLY CONSIDERED TO BE SEAPLANE PARADISE.

A Noorduyn Norseman Mk V of Red Lake Airways is moored alongside the quay at Red Lake, Ontario, with a De Havilland Canada DHC-2 Beaver seaplane in the background.

The De Havilland Canada DHC-3 Otter of Green Airways moves away from the shore to take off from Red Lake in June 1990.

A Grumman Turbo-Mallard belonging to Chalk's, America's oldest airline, waits for its passengers on Miami's 'seadrome' situated in the heart of the city.

A Grumman G-73T Turbo-Mallard (below) of the Virgin Islands Shuttle leaves the port of St Thomas in February 1989.

Close-up of the 600hp Pratt & Whitney Wasp engines (right) of a G-73 that has not been modified to take turboprops.

FLORIDA

From the Chalk's terminal situated on Watson Island, Miami, it is possible to go to the Bahamas and to the island of Bimini with its enchanting landscapes, flying in a Grumman Turbo-Mallard or an Albatross. The flying boats also take tourists to the Virgin Islands.

Moored off a beach at Key West, a Chalk's Turbo-Mallard displays its new livery in March 1993.

The largest flying boat transport built by Grumman is the G-111 Albatross.

They are based on reconditioned military machines. This Chalk's flying boat is parked under palm trees on the island of Bimini.

A Grumman Turbo-Mallard, with its landing gear lowered, about to climb onto the specially prepared foreshore of St Thomas Island.
The Grumman amphibians maintain the tradition of the Pan American flying boats.

Float biplanes still in working order are extremely rare.
This Waco YKC, photographed at Anchorage in 1989, is one of the survivors.

The De Havilland Canada DHC-6 is the largest float seaplane.
This machine belonging to Sound Adventures Air Service is being checked over at Lake Hood in Alaska. It can carry 20 passengers or 2 tons of freight.

ALASKA
One of the most attractive seaplane museums is at Anchorage in Alaska. It is possible to reach Juneau by seaplane, and then Lake Hood, from where the views of the mountains are particularly spectacular.

Helio have fitted floats to several of their aircraft.
This five-seater is not only very smart, but also able to take off in a very short distance. Even so it has not succeeded in becoming a serious competitor for the Cessnas.

A De Havilland Canada DHC-2 seaplane at Juneau in June 1989 (far left).
This aircraft is used as a small 'flying truck'.

The DHC-2 Beavers (left) are often chartered by small transport companies.
This one was photographed at Lake Hood.

Like the aircraft converted into seaplanes in North America, this Cessna 206 Stationair has floats made by EDO .

The Beech D-18S of Rusty Myers
Flying Service flies over a
typical landscape in north-
western Canada, where there
are countless lakes.

This De Havilland Canada DHC-
6 Twin Otter belongs to BC Air.
It is manoeuvring on the waters of
Lake Ketchikan in June 1987.

A Sportsman Airways DHC-3 Otter alights at a good angle on Fort Frances Lake.
When the weather is fine, the Canadian seaplanes fly anglers to areas which are not otherwise accessible.

The shark's mouth is an odd decoration for a civil aircraft.
Rusty Myers none the less chose it to adorn his Beeches, no doubt as a reminder that they served in the Second World War.

CANADA

British Columbia, and even more so, Ontario, have remarkable networks of rivers and lakes which mean they are truly paradise for the seaplane enthusiast. The seaplanes also enable anglers to gain access to wild and beautiful places.

Temesco Airlines uses DHC-3s on Misty Fjord, a departure point for large cruise ships.

(Insets)

Beech 18S, registration C-GEHX, warms up its engines on Red Lake, Ontario before taking to the air (far left).

A Cessna Skywagon II belonging to Harbour Air about to take off in Vancouver Harbour (above left).

One can count up to a hundred seaplanes at the same time at this one seaplane harbour. Such views of another age make the north-west of Canada into a seaplane paradise (above).

A general view of Red Lake taken in June 1990.

Built in New Orleans and delivered to the U.S. Navy in 1945, this Consolidated PBY-6A CC-CNP is used as a water-bomber by Aeroservicio Paragué in Chile. It is warming up its engines on Rodelillo airfield.

186

OTHER PLACES

In Hawaii or in Chile, in California or in Austria amphibious seaplanes are still to be found in use. Even today they offer an ideal mode of transport for getting to places that are difficult to reach by any other means. Apart from being useful in this way, the seaplane, by providing an unusual view of these exceptionally beautiful parts of the world, becomes an indispensable tool of modern tourism. Most of the seaplanes used were built during or just after the Second World War. Their old-fashioned appearance adds to the fascination exerted by these great buzzing insects, which rise into the sky after ploughing their double furrow across the surface of the water. Today seaplanes are associated with leisure, and in the rugged individualism of those who use them is to be found the last survival of the adventure of marine aviation.

A probably unique survivor of the German shipboard seaplane force from the Second World War, this Arado Ar 196A-3 (above) belongs to Krumovo Museum in Bugaria, where it was photographed in 1993.

Surprise in Hawaii: the strangely shaped Republic RC-3 Seabee (above left).
This amphibian, of which more than a thousand were built just after the war, was supposed to be an all-purpose machine, but its promoters' optimism was exaggerated.

This Widgeon, used by Heli Air, warms up its engines on the runway at Innsbruck in October 1990 (above right).
The aircraft was built in France by the S.C.A.N. under licence from Grumman.

This Royal Navy Grumman J4F-2 Gosling 1 has been restored in its original colours in Chino, California.
Gosling was the name used by the British for the Widgeon.

INDEX

A BC Air DHC-6 Otter.

188

**A Green Airways
DHC-3 Otter.**

A Green Airways Beech 3 NM (D-18S).

A Green Airways Beech 3 NM (D-18S).

PHOTOGRAPHIC CREDITS

Musée de l'Air et de l'Espace : pages 8, 9, 11(t), 12, 13(t), 15(t), 16(t)(b)(b), 17, 18, 19(t)(b), 20(t)(b)(b), 21, 22(t)(r), 23(t)(b), 24(t), 25(l)(r), 26, 27, 28(t)(br)(bl), 29(t)(b), 30(t)(b), 31(t)(m)(b), 32, 33(t)(m)(b), 34(t)(bl)(br), 35(t)(m)(b), 36, 37, 43(b)

Air France : pages, 80, 81, 82, 83, 84,
Borgé : pages, 50, 51, 93, 108, 109
Canadair : pages, 170, 171, 172
Caproni : page 92
Claudius Dornier : page 173
Convair : pages 131, 132, 133, 134, 135, 144, 148, 159, 160, 161
Curtiss : pages 57, 70, 138
Devaux : pages 10, 11, 24, 38, 39, 40, 41, 42, 43, 46, 47, 53, 58, 59, 60, 61
Delmas : pages 156, 157, 158, 160, 161
Dornier : pages 39, 72, 73, 85, 87, 88, 89, 90, 91, 111, 116, 125, 126
Douglas : page 71
Evain : pages 174, 175, 176, 177, 178, 179, 180, 181, 182, 183, 184, 185, 186, 187, 188
Ginter : pages 64, 65, 66, 67, 68, 69
Gorokoff : page 49
Grumman : pages 62, 76, 166, 167
Guigui : page 173
Hughes : pages 154, 155
Junkers : page 85
Lockheed : page 78
Macchi : pages 63, 93
Marrand : pages 112, 113, 114, 115, 117, 119, 120, 121, 127, 138, 149, 150, 151, 152, 153, 164
Marani : pages 13, 14 , 15, 24, 44, 45, 52
Martin : pages 140, 146, 147, 162, 163, 165
Mikesh : pages 48, 136, 137, 139, 141
Müller : pages 112, 113, 118, 128, 129, 142, 143
Pan Am : pages 77, 100, 101, 102, 103, 104, 105, 106, 107
Service historique de l'armée de l'air : pages 55, 56
Shin Meïwa : pages 168, 169
Short : pages 94, 95, 96, 97, 122, 123, 124, 146
Sikorsky : page 79